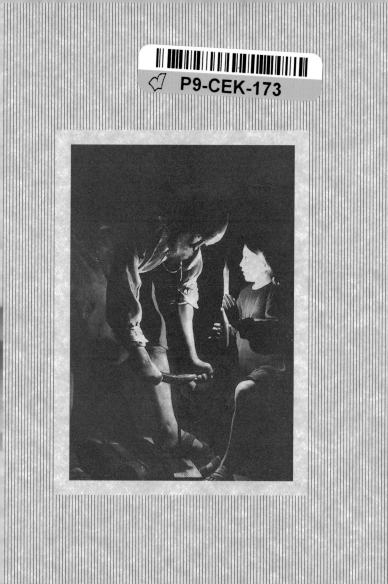

Once again
To My Special
Friend who always
inspires me. I Love You!

Mary Mueller Murphy Schwath

ILLUMINATA

MARIANNE WILLIAMSON

ILLUMINATA

Thoughts, Prayers,
Rites of Passage

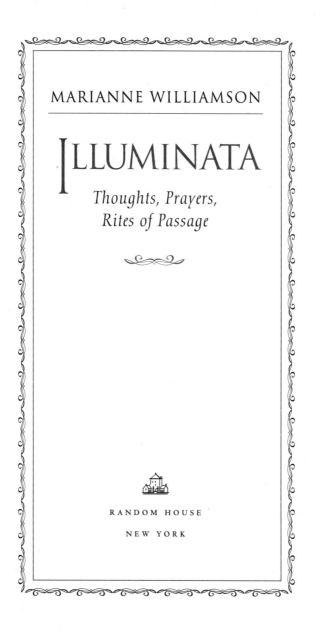

RANDOM HOUSE

NEW YORK

Library of Congress Catalog Card Number: 94-67888

Manufactured in the United States of America
9 8 7 6 5 4 3

Book design by J. K. Lambert

For

Diane Meyer Simon

My heartfelt thanks to
Gregorio Vlastelica, Ian Patrick, Mark Adams,
Max Dowling, Jeremy Walters, Carrie Rose,
Kenny D'Cruz, and Ansal Trafford,
whose work and ideas were the seeds of this book.

I am deeply grateful
to all the many, many people throughout the world
who have shared with me
your thoughts and your own prayers for light.

A WAY IN

I see in my mind a little ball of golden light.
I watch this light as it begins to grow larger and
　　larger, until now it covers the entire inner
　　vision of my mind.
I see within this light a beautiful temple.
I see a garden that surrounds the temple and a
　　body of water that flows through the garden.
I see that the inside of the temple is lit by this
　　same beautiful golden light, and I am here,
For I have been drawn here by the power and in
　　the presence of God.
I dedicate my days and my relationships and
　　experiences to You.
May Your Spirit, which is within me, so guide
　　my thoughts, my feelings and my perceptions
　　of all things
That I might grow into a happier, more peace-
　　ful, more loving human being.
Illumine my mind, illumine my life.
Amen.

CONTENTS

INTRODUCTION

A mass movement is afoot in the world today,
spiritual in nature and radical in its implications.
After decades of declining influence on the
affairs of the world, there is once again a
widespread consideration of spiritual principles
as an antidote to the pain of our times. Like
flowers growing up through pieces of broken
cement, signs of hope and faith appear everywhere. These signs reflect the light of a transcendent force at the center of things, present in our
lives in a corrective and even miraculous manner,
a light we can reach personally through internal
work of a devotional nature. We are experiencing
now an alteration of collective consciousness,
centered not in government or science or religion
per se. It is centered nowhere because it is present, at least potentially, everywhere. It is the rising up of our true divine nature, a reassertion of
God in the consciousness of modern man.

Beneath the dramas of a changeable world lies

what physicists call a unified field. This field, the wellspring of all possibilities, is not visible to the physical eye. We know that its components exist not because we can measure them (we cannot, for they are too small), but because we see the trails they leave in their wake. On the other hand, when we are not observing these components, they leave no trails. It is the very act of putting our attention on these elements that calls them into existence.

How like this is to the observation of religious rites. "Do you observe the holidays?" someone asks. What this actually means is, Do you observe the holiness of this day, that through the creative act of your observation, the day might be made holy for you? How profound a realization it is: the power of our own perception to influence the nature of life experience.

We see God when we observe Him. When we do not put our attention on Him, we do not see the effects of His existence. It is in consciously observing Him that we create a world in which there are holy things to be observed. This book is an effort to create a context for the observation of God, that we might see Him more clearly and call forth His power more perfectly in our lives.

PART ONE

THOUGHTS

"If you bring forth what is within you, what you bring forth will save you. If you do not bring forth what is within you, what you do not bring forth will destroy you."

as attributed to Jesus Christ in
The Gospel of Thomas

· 1 ·

Renaissance

There is a spiritual renaissance sweeping the world. It is a revolution in the way we think. Most people feel it, some deride it, many embrace it and no one can stop it.

Its torchbearers are a motley mix. Some are religious in a traditional sense, while some are not. Some are successful in the world, while some are not. Some of us genuinely like one another, while some of us do not. Some are politically liberal, while some of us are conservative. Some seek Truth in fellowship and some seek Truth alone. Some of us are old and some of us are young.

We are an assorted group, an unlabeled group, but together in spirit, we are affecting the world in significant ways. We are turning away from a purely worldly orientation. We seek an ancient God and a modern God. We feel a current of change, a cosmic electricity that runs through our veins. However disparate our personalities and interests, we all agree on one very important point: Mankind has come to a major crossroads, at which the spirit alone can lead us toward human survival.

We wage, in our way, a revolution based on love. We seek to replace an old, oppressive order, not so much politically or socially, but within our minds where it lives and works. We try to hate no one, for we recognize that hatred itself is the enemy. We hope to change the world into a place of grace and love.

The first shots have rung out in this revolution, and they were not shots. They were bursts of light, streaming silently yet dramatically through the hearts and minds of millions. This historic unfoldment has already begun, and it is playing out on inner planes.

The question on most people's minds, whether conscious or unconscious, is this: What

will happen now? From channeled entities claiming to hail from the Pleiades to fundamentalist
Christians, from the prophecies of Nostradamus
to visions of the Virgin Mary, from angels who
whisper to a backwoods carpenter to scientific
think tanks, come predictions of global shift,
perhaps cataclysm, in the years ahead. Our own
inner sense corroborates the evidence: It doesn't
seem as though the future is going to be much like
the past. It feels as though something is up, as
though something significant and big is about to
occur.

It feels, for one thing, as though something is
fundamentally wrong. It isn't just the environment,
just the wars, just the gangs or the violence or the
drugs. It isn't just the lack of values or integrity
or love. Something lurks. In Yeats's poem "The
Second Coming," he describes a time in which
the center cannot hold. Our center isn't holding.
The center isn't there.

And yet, the deeper the despair that seems to
creep around the edges of things, the brighter the
light that seems to beckon from the center. It
turns out that the center only seemed not to be
there; it has merely been ignored. To those who
look inward, it is bright indeed. Now, in growing

intensity and yearning, the mind of humanity is seeking its Source.

The antidote to what is fundamentally wrong is the cultivation of what is fundamentally right. Should we choose to expand who we are on a fundamental level, new structures will replace the casualties of premillennial disintegration, and the next twenty years will usher in an age of light more dazzling than the world has known. The next twenty years will be the deciding factor. We need all our attention and all our focus to turn the species in the direction of survival.

Ultimately, the choice to love each other is the only choice for a survivable future. The meek shall inherit the earth because everyone else will have died on their swords. Every time we open our hearts, we create the space for a global alternative.

The opening of the heart is an awesome personal politic, providing us with an internal strength greater than any worldly power. As we receive God's love and impart it to others, we are given the power to repair the world. As we give up our collective enslavement to the dictates of Western materialism, we relinquish the increasingly primitive belief that the world outside remains unaffected by our thoughts. We have begun to recognize that our individual minds create our collective realities, and we are ready to take responsibility for the world by taking more seriously our individual contributions to it. Personal transformation can and does have global effects. As we go, so goes the world, for the world *is* us. The revolution that will save the world is ultimately a personal one.

Some people think that things are no worse now than they have ever been, that all this talk of some millennial shift is nonsense, even danger-ous. Perhaps this book is not for them. I am not trying to convince anyone of the reality of a global crisis; I am concerned, as are millions of others, with increasing consensus and hope among those who already believe that there is one.

This is the drama of our times: the climax of our historical epoch, as we reach the conclusion of the twentieth century. Our planet, our species, our generation is shifting. And they are all the same shift. This is not a personal story, though everyone's personal life is affected and everyone's life affects the story. Like strands of DNA, all of us are coded with the history and possibilities of the species. Ours is a collective, generational drama, for our dramas at their core are all the same story. We all came from the angels and we have all fallen far. Now we are poised on the edge of a cliff. As a group, we will fall, or as a group we will fly.

The 1990s are a power point in time, an opening in a revolving door that last passed this way in the 1960s. Now, as then, we have a limited time in which to jump in. The decade of the sixties was a societal peak experience, a red-letter era in our evolutionary journey. It was a premystical phase, which foreshadowed current history. An entire generation of souls was marked for a lifetime by having experienced that period. Like Cinderella, who retained one glass slipper even after the spell broke, which then gave her entrance back into the magic, we have retained our cultural talismans and waited three decades for reentrance to a state of collective hope. We had a glimpse of an expanded reality, however drug-based that glimpse might have been at the time. Much as we receive the mark of a rubber stamp on our hands when we enter a place of entertainment, indicating that we don't *have* to reenter but we *can*, an entire generation now looks at that stamp on our hands and wonders if maybe we had it figured out right back then after all. We were marked, chemically altered by those days, and however far we might have run from them, they have never stopped haunting us. We are beckoned by the music, the philosophies, the pictures, the personalities. No one who was not there then can imagine the way our souls were branded. And they were branded for a reason: Now that we have begun to awaken from the sleep of two ultramaterialistic decades, the branding on our souls, on our hands, sparks our memory. We are jarred by what we know.

We are not the only generation waking. Everyone on earth at this time is permeated with the vibrations of a closing chapter in a historical cycle. Small electrical shocks pulse through our nervous systems. We are coded with the knowledge that at this point we must change our course. Memories come from the future as well as the past. The twentysomething generation has a complementary metaphysics to that of the baby boomers, harking as we did to sounds the world can't hear. Generations are like keys on a piano; baby boomers and twentysomethings are a musical perfect third.

We are a ragamuffin group in many ways, but great revolutions have begun with less.

There is a feeling in the air now, a sense, however faint, of renewed magic. The nineties seem to be revving up for something. We have arrived full circle at the point where we began this journey in the sixties, but this time, those who carry the torch are sober. We began, in those days, a collective quest for an enlightened perspective, and now, perhaps, we might actually find it. Our sobriety is more total than mere recovery from addiction to drugs and alcohol. A genuinely sober life is one in which moderation is embraced as a higher good, for the valuable part it plays in the creation and right use of energy. We're letting go our addictions to many things: to people, to sex, to worldly illusions. Those who are not sober today risk missing the train of history. Sobriety itself is today's high, for it is ultimately in the most centered consciousness that we find our power to transcend the world.

We are looking not so much for more ground to conquer, but for a truer ground of being on which to stand inside ourselves. The most positive breakthroughs of our times are internal. The drama of personal actualization is rarely reported in the popular press, except in irreverent, often ignorant tones. What is the story, after all? The story is an inner drama, in a world beneath the surface of things. When the eyes are closed, light isn't seen. Still it works its miraculous transformations. Both men and women are becoming more authentic and powerful, as the light within us intensifies. We are beginning to see ourselves in a new perspective, to generations before and after us, to the earth, to each other, to God. We are beginning to recognize simultaneously our many human weaknesses and our many divine strengths.

This is the zeitgeist of our times: a turning inward of the Western mind. After centuries of looking to the outer world for our solace and power, we have begun to see the limits of a primarily external orientation. We see how much we have sacrificed, how disempowered we have all become, looking to worldly institutions for the answers that lie inside us. We've embraced cold, technical, mechanistic reasoning (not that those are embraceable things), and suppressed our most essential strengths: passion, intuition, sense of the sacred, prophecy, vision and healing. And thus we have been controlled, by thoughts, by institutions, by all manner of illusion.

The history of the world is the history of control—by institutions, individuals and ideas— over masses of people who finally rise up against the control and then avoid, or not, the temptation to try to control others as they were once controlled. Seizing someone's soul is the ultimate form of control, because without the soul we are without our love. Without our love, we're without our power. In this sense, we are as controlled a society as has ever existed, for the soul has been grossly peripheralized here.

Now the slaves are beginning to agitate. We're starting at last to honor our own discomfort, to think that maybe we weren't crazy after all, chafing for years under the oppressive weight of all our cultural nonsense. Millions of us now reach out for our lost, buried souls, and once we begin the search, we're bound to find it. The game has been to keep us from looking, by constantly attracting our eyes to something else, by invalidating our personal radar. But we're starting to see that game for what it is, to see where it's led us. There's no one to blame, but we must all take responsibility for a quick and fundamental change.

Only the most bitter and cynical among us still cling to the dreams of a soulless world, but their influence is waning, their power now almost ghostly. We must not let their screams, however agonized, sarcastic and loud they might be, deter us from our revolutionary goal. We must respect ourselves enough, at last, to absolutely know what we know. Something is wrong. We feel it. We must hold to the conviction that the heart, not the brain, is the light of the world. The mind goes insane without the guidance of the heart. The intellect must bow to the spiritual impulse. We have been impregnated by a divine idea, and out of the womb of our mature consideration will come, when the time is ripe, the birthing of a better world. We are preparing to give birth to the people we are meant to be.

We are here to invoke a global renaissance, as deeply transformative of human civilization as was the Renaissance that followed the Middle

Ages. Dominated by two world wars that cast their webs of suffering over the mass of humanity, the twentieth century has had its darkness and perversity as well as its light. As we end this century and prepare for the new, our greatest power to affect the world lies in our capacity to forgive and release what has been and surrender what shall be into the hands of God. It is that surrender and release that constitute the renaissance of history and the resurrection of the fallen human race.

In April 1994, Richard Nixon died. In May, John Smith, the leader of Britain's Labour party, died in London. Several days later, Jacqueline Kennedy Onassis died. These passings marked the end of an era, not only for these two countries but for others as well. The generation that wielded Western power during the post–World War II era has begun not only retiring to the wings but literally leaving the theater. Those of us who follow them now stand in front of history's spotlight whether we are comfortable there or not, whether we are ready to perform or remain hopelessly unprepared.

Every age has its members who watch the show of history from the sidelines. In fact, the majority of people usually do. But there is within every generation a group will to survive and to move the drama of human history forward. This generation, despite our guilt, our shame, and our narcissism, has as much to give as any other, perhaps more so, since we have given so little until now compared to what we are capable of giving. We will do more than move history forward: In fact, we will redefine history. For we will usher in the posthistoric era, redefining the meaning of time by fundamentally rising above it. We will reach the climax of our millennium, take a very deep breath and exhale a world born new. We will do these things because we must: We will spiritually mutate in order to save the human race.

I have heard it said that the earth is being bombarded by huge amounts of electromagnetic energy, a bombardment that then expresses itself in droughts, floods, earthquakes and volcanoes. Anyone who has ever witnessed a child's growth, who has seen a woman move through the phases of pregnancy or has been pregnant herself knows the enormous amount of energy released when life pushes against its boundaries. Life perpetuates itself through energetic outburst, much as an engine turns over when being turned on. The

earth, which reflects our moods in ways the
ancients understood but the modern mind has
forgotten, is now bursting forth in seemingly
chaotic ways. It is trying to grow. It is trying to
return to paradise. It is trying to shake off the
toxins of our miscreations, physical and emotional. It will propel humanity into our next
phase of development, whether the transition
before us is easy or not. These fearful so-called
earth changes are actually the earth expressing
itself dangerously when we have chosen not to
express ourselves creatively.

We have the power to affect those changes, to
harness the energy of the earth and turn its out-
bursts into positive expression, because the
energy of the earth is also within us. The ways of
worship, of genuine spiritual devotion, are rites
by which we alchemize our world both within
and without. As we transform the energies inside
ourselves, we transform the energies of earth.
This is how Moses parted the Red Sea. As we
pray and meditate and actualize our highest
potential, we become shock absorbers for the
excess electromagnetic energy that bombards the
planet. If we do this en masse, the earth will calm

down. However, if we do not meet this challenge to find once more our connection to God, the earth will reflect our resistance to growth. It will do what it has to do to bring us to our senses. It will do what it has to do to bring us to our knees.

This is not talk of doom but of the critical choices that face us. Our environment now threatens us as we have threatened it, through internal as well as external pollution. Acid rain singes the earth and hatred singes the soul. Only spirit can handle the heat. Only love can counter the hatred that has metastasized like cancer, eating away at humanity from Sarajevo to Rwanda to the streets of the United States. There is no form of government enlightened enough, no legislation powerful enough, no army or police force strong enough to contain the forces of darkness unleashed by global hatred. It's as though Hitler was a tumor, and we hoped that with the end of World War II we had gotten out all the cancer. But we didn't and it's spreading now, at a rate so fast that only the chance of instantaneous remission offers any hope for humanity at all. Hatred itself is the problem; not this group or that group. Hatred itself is the cancer that threatens the survival of the species. The only antidote is spiritual. The only medicine is love.

We must stop looking to our leaders to bolster our mass denial. We must not perpetuate the illusion that the right government, the right technology, or the right armies can fix our problems. They cannot. We must ask our leaders to help us give up our mass denial and get down on their knees along with us, that all of us might pray to God to do what only God can do.

God is a peaceful ground of being. He is the energy of nonviolence. To ask Him to help us is to ask Him to turn us into profoundly peaceful people. Only a massive intention to embrace the ways of nonviolence—in families, government, business, entertainment, in any and every way that such an intention could express itself—can propel humanity beyond the trajectory toward its own destruction. We are like a missile that must change course. We must exert the energy it takes to change our direction in midstream. Every single one of us is necessary to create the force field that will lead us into species reversal. With every prayer and every thought of love, we release the light that will cast out darkness. One light alone seems small and weak, but no one's light is ever alone, for all our lights are part of God. We are bolstered by Him and by each other. We are not just soldiers. We're a revolution.

Peace is much more than the absence of war and violence; it is a condition unto itself. There is more to being healthy than the absence of illness, and there is more to peace than the absence of war. We can't fight war without warring. Our goal at this point must be the *creation* of peace. Without love, there is no peace. Where love is absent, war of some kind is inevitable. Let us be very clear, as we sign our names to the invisible declaration of independence from the ways of war: The commitment to love is treasonous to the ways of the world. War does not threaten the status quo; in many ways it bolsters it. Only love is a threat to the established order, for love really changes things. Only love breaks all the way through.

Mentally, we have exiled love. We have relegated it to narrow regions of social dialogue. It is considered a relevant conversation between a husband and a wife, for instance, but not between a government and its people. It's fine for the bedroom but not for the classroom. This is totally insane. Our emotional development has not kept pace with our material progress. Our modes of thinking have not kept pace with our technologies. We wouldn't dream of using outmoded building techniques to build a skyscraper, but our mental techniques are outmoded indeed. We can send a man to the moon but we can't keep peace in our families and neighborhoods. That is because the former task does not demand compassion.

The human species has all but lost its heart; we gave it up for the illusionary fruits of the material world. But a life without heart is a life without life force. The psyche, as well as the body, needs both heart and brain in order to survive. Like Chinese women who bound their feet and then could no longer walk freely, we have bound our hearts, and thus stunted our growth as moral beings.

We must be about our Father's business, which means the business of our Source, which is love and love only. Anything loving that we do or think contributes to the healing of humanity.

Any turning away from love literally holds back the planet. We are perched on the brink of a miraculous transition from the ways of fear to the ways of love. Having seen enough darkness, we're attracted to the light. We're eyeing the keys to the kingdom. We're picking them up. We're using their power.

Every loving thought we think is a powerful key to the kingdom. Through prayer, meditation, and the silence of a profound holiness, we refocus our dispersed and irresponsible thought forms. We thus take up the challenge to redirect world history. We must relinquish our passive observation of the world outside; we can open the door to the world we want. In understanding ourselves, we come to understand the world. In allowing ourselves to heal, we become the healers of the world. In praying for peace, we become bringers of peace. Thus we actualize the power within us to remedy the psychic wounds of humanity.

Spiritual practice heals us, bringing down light to the regions of our darkness. We need more than brilliant analysis; we need a miracle. The human mind can't give us that, but the human mind isn't all we've got. The human mind contains a spark of divinity, and that divinity illumines us. The illumined mind has transcended worldly illusion. It's so drawn to the light that it merges with the light. And in that merger lies the hope for mankind.

The Luminous Mind

Illumination is light in the mind, the Word made flesh, the integration of heaven and earth. It is abstract principle dressed in human cloth, the light-filled explosion that occurs when the mind has embraced its Source. Illumination is not of this world. It lifts us above the lies of the world by helping us to detach from them. Illumination is both our source and our destiny, the reason we came here and the reason we stay.

We are here to achieve an uplifted mode of being. We are meant to return to the living light, which casts out the darkness of our mental miscreations.

Illumination is a deepening sense of the sacred. It is the spiritual laser that cuts through the blocks to our liberation. Liberation, or breakthrough, is actually a movement into ourselves, the door to the next phase of our evolutionary journey.

Pharaoh's enslavement of the Jews and his refusal to let them out of Egypt is a biblical symbol for the ego's unjust and hateful attempts to violate the spirit. Moses represents divine consciousness, telling Pharaoh, "Let my people go." When Pharaoh refused to do so, God sent disasters to persuade him to change his mind. So it is that the disasters that now threaten the earth are not our punishment but actually warnings to the ego. It must give up its pernicious control and let our spirits fly free.

Moses led his people out of Egypt, just as the spirit leads us out of bondage. The period of time between leaving Egypt and reaching the promised land, as well as the period between the Crucifixion and the Resurrection, represent the passage out of darkness into light. Illumination is the building of the passage, the construction of the spiritual tunnel through which the soul finds its way out of ego-bound darkness into mystical light. Illumination is not metaphor but reality. Its light, although rarely seen by the human eye, is an actual force of destruction and creation. It is the building block of the new world as well as the destroyer of the old.

God's truth is literal truth. The illumined mind has more operative cells. In reclaiming the mystical, we take back our whole selves. Formerly barren mental lands spring to new life through the planting of spiritual seeds. We must plant now and we must harvest. Einstein once said we would never solve the problems of the world from the level of thinking we were at when we created them.

We are on the brink of an important break-through in human consciousness. The very prevalence of planetary darkness at this time is but a sign that the negative ego is threatened, sensing the danger to its existence and fighting for its survival. The torch that is borne by the human heart, by everyone who loves or who even believes that there is such a thing as love, casts a light in whose presence the darkness of the world cannot continue to exist. We must believe, we must hold on to this, we must do our part to let the rays of light shine through us. Our lack of conviction holds back the world. Our willingness to serve it opens up the windows and lets light stream in.

The universe works with a more varied palette than do the venues of power and influence acknowledged by the world. The universe is like an infinitely powerful computer, registering a spark of willingness on anyone's part to receive the light and then impart it to others. As we pray and meditate, attuning our hearts and minds to God, we become universal channels for the power of good. Our own luminosity is the potent yet passive element in a complete creative process: It prepares the ground for positive materialization. Luminosity is the feminine aspect of consciousness, the spiritual yin to the physical yang.

The luminous mind has a quantum effect. It doesn't have a practical influence in ways the world can always see. It ultimately produces practical effects, but not necessarily in a linear fashion, a way the left brain can track. A friend of mine recently returned from a trip to Tibet. She visited with a Buddhist monk while there, and at the end of their time together, he said to her simply, "It isn't rational."

Luminosity is our miracle-readiness, a mental and emotional preparedness for service. God is alert to our readiness for use. His greatest desire is to alchemize our being, that He might then send us out as His lamps unto the world. The Lord Krishna of the Hindu religion says in his sermon called the Bhagavad Gita, "Whenever virtue subsides and immorality prevails, then I body Myself forth. For the protection of the good, for the destruction of the wicked, and for the establishment of Dharma [righteousness], I come into being, in every age." He comes into being through us.

Luminosity is the power of the mind to influence the world in a positive way. It radiates invisible energies, unspoken commands, which have the effect of awakening the higher mind in others. In the movie *Schindler's List*, the character of Schindler's accountant, played by Ben Kingsley, demonstrates this luminosity: Barred by circumstances from fully speaking his opinions, the man's moral substance has a profound effect on Schindler nevertheless. This change within Schindler saves many people's lives. Philosophically, the accountant is the center of the movie, the miracle-worker, the conduit of truth, the bearer of a silent power that casts out evil through the awakening of good.

It is, in fact, the darkness of the world that calls up the light. Just as a sloppy room makes you wish someone would clean it, and a messy room might even make you contemplate *paying* someone to clean it, a severely messy room makes you get up and do it yourself, for the mess is impairing your ability to happily live here. There is a *desire* then, where before there was a mere unfocused "Wouldn't it be nice." This is the anatomy of a civilization that reinvents itself. We want to do what we have not done. We want to produce not just marvelous machines or marvelous systems, but marvelous people who bring down the light.

We are, in this sense, no different than the people of any other age. From the trough in the water comes the rising of the wave. We are the wave now rising, and the fact that we have been so low increases the chances that our surge will be filled with awesome power.

There is, at this time, a reaching out to the species, through deep subterranean caverns of divine action. God calls to us and our listening grows. He has always called but we have rarely listened. Now, as our yearning reaches critical mass, there are millions of human hands cupped to human ears, listening for the sounds of God. We have heard something beautiful. We want to hear more.

We want an alchemical transformation of the experience of being human. That is what true religion is. Anthropologists have found that people began creating religions at the same time they began creating works of art. The desire for transcendence is inherent in who we are, for the earth as we know it is a hard and nonmiraculous place. There is nothing in this world that can truly give us peace, for peace lies in our transcendence of this world. Our most fervent wish is for the peace of God.

We receive His peace when we ask Him for it. We keep His peace by extending it to others. Those are the keys and there are no others.

Spiritual wisdom is now available to everyone, disseminated to the masses as never before in world history. Finally, a few trips to the library, and we have a pretty good sense of what *all* the masters said. They all said the same things. There is a mass discovery that Jesus is truth, the Torah is truth, Mohammed is truth, Krishna is truth, Buddha is truth, and so on. They are all truth and they are all among us now. The New Jerusalem means the unification of the world's spiritual traditions. We live, as theologian Matthew Fox has said, in a "post-denominational age." The great religious figures are psychic realities as real as anything physical or material around us, and our openness to them will free our minds. The learning of the world too often deadens instead of frees us.

We are now at the crossroads of two huge, divergent points of view: One is materialistic and one is mystical. One is worldly and one is holy. One is based on fear of the world and one has fallen in love.

I used to think I was not religious, and perhaps I was not. I didn't like what organized religion had done to the world. I still do not. I have come to see, however, that true religion is internal, not external. The spirit within us cannot be blamed for the blasphemies carried out in its name. What some have done in the name of religion, projecting their neuroses, even perpetrating evil on the world, does not make religion as a mystical phenomenon invalid. In fact, nothing could be so relevant or so necessary in the world today, as that we might carve out an inner kingdom for ourselves, dwell there with God and be cleansed.

Secularized organized religions have become, in many cases, as calcified as other institutions that form the structure of our modern world. That's why they are accepted here, and also why they are rejected. Our religious institutions have far too often become handmaidens of the status quo, while the genuine religious experience is anything but that. True religion is by nature disruptive of what has been, giving birth to the eternally new. It is subtly revolutionary, for love by its nature is radical and ecstatic. It's a force by which we burst out from what is old and calcified, into a higher mode of being. The internal experience of true religion is the process by which the human being breaks out of his bondage into full, free spirit. Within that freedom, there is no consciousness of slavery, nor respect for any structure that seeks to limit or control us.

The genuine religious impulse, the fiery passion at the center of things, is as suspect now as it has ever been, for self-actualized people are hard to manipulate, difficult to control. Genuine religion does not respect the world, for it sees right through it. Its goal is to supplant the world with something much more beautiful.

A friend of Abraham Lincoln once remarked about him, "He's so religious he's beyond religion."

Experience of the spirit breaks through illusions of our guilt and separateness. It is radically committed to the natural goodness and inherent oneness that lie at the center of who we really are.

Religious institutions, as such, are not the only arbiters of religious experience. They do not own the Truth, for Truth cannot be owned. Nor should they think they hold some franchise on our spiritual life. They are consultants and frameworks, but they are not God Himself. We should not confuse the path with the destination.

It is simplistic to think that many Americans turned away from organized religion and now we're back, as though that's the whole story. We turned away from religion, found that life without conscious awareness of God is difficult, and we're now back to religion because that is, theoretically, where to find Him. But we do not go back as the spiritually half-interested, complacent congregants that many of our parents were when we were growing up. We go back with an interest in actually *having* a religious experience. Organized religion will not be the same; it will step up to bat, religiously, or it will wither away. Organized religious institutions are in for a huge transformation, for the simple reason that people have become genuinely religious in spite of them.

Spirituality is an inner fire, a mystical sustenance that feeds our souls. The mystical journey drives us into ourselves, to a sacred flame at our center. The purpose of the religious experience is to develop the eyes by which we see this inner flame, and our capacity to live its mystery. In its presence, we are warmed and ignited. When too far from the blaze, we are cold and spiritually lifeless. We are less than human without that heat. Our connection to God is life itself.

Religion means "to bind back." Its purpose is to turn us back into ourselves, to the well inside from which we are endlessly creative. God is a well that does not run dry. Religion is the process by which we constantly check in with God, as a child checks in with her mother. Once she feels secure, she is free to roam and wander. So do we need the constant reassurance that we are loved and protected, guided and watched over. Then we have the strength and self-esteem we need to show up fearlessly in a fearful world.

Living in a society that undervalues the spirit, we who embrace it are tempted to apologize for our interest. We must stop apologizing, for no subject is more important. It is, after all, love's retrieval. It is the answer to global hatred. To invalidate the spiritual life is to shoot at the fire-man who is putting out the fire.

The more we turn to God and ask Him to use us for His purposes, the more the mind expands and illumines. We experience the peace of God more deeply and the joy of our natural innocence more often, as we apply a genuinely religious commitment to all we think and do. The spiritual commitment is to make every situation an object of devotional connection.

When we do this, something miraculous happens. I know this firsthand, for I have seen in my work a glimpse of something that is out of the ordinary. When I'm working, I'm not a different person, but I think I become a more *able* one. I feel lifted up when I lecture. It feels as though my mind is expanded, as though my emotional abilities are greater than they normally are. I feel more centered in my strengths, as though I've entered a mental and emotional gulf stream.

I know that many others have felt this same upliftment: Therapists, healers, clergy and transformational facilitators report the same kind of temporarily expanded abilities. Most artists and creative people know of this experiential vortex. It's like we're given a mystical helmet, and all of a sudden we feel we can fly.

Albert Einstein once described his creative moments as "muscular." There's a consciousness we're capable of that integrates our various dimensions. It's joyful to be there because it feels like we've broken through constrictions which normally hold us back. This kind of spontaneous integration is not so out of the ordinary, so much as it is not a part of ordinary conversation. It is underdiscussed and underinvestigated, invalidated as too soft or even ridiculed as nonsense. Although defined in psychology as "peak experience" and in physics as the "flow," this integrated consciousness is rarely appreciated for the opportunity it offers, to lead us up and out of our universal morass. The spiritual life is a high-energy phenomenon in a very tired world. It's outside the limits of the secular box that dominates our social dialogue. Mystical thought is trivialized, diminished, even labeled inane by our gatekeepers, but spiritual concepts are breaking into the vernacular despite the resistance of a materialistic bias. Those who obstruct the spiritual conversation are standing in the way of an urgently needed unfoldment. Science will one day validate the mystical experience—in fact it has already begun to do so—but this waiting around for science to tell us that the sky is blue is becoming an increasingly unacceptable slowing down of the spiritual wagon train. Who's giving permission to whom? The mystical experience doesn't need the world at all, but the world desperately needs the mystical experience.

During the Renaissance of the sixteenth and seventeenth centuries, I doubt that many people walking down the street turned to each other and said, "This is the Renaissance, don't you think?" But looking back, we're clear there was one. We are changing now, bursting forth in ways we don't know how to describe. We must not think something doesn't exist or isn't important just because it isn't languaged. The mystical impulse is beyond words, but it is liberating itself from the bondage of our limited thinking. It is breaking out of the quiet chamber in our hearts. Like blood, it flows *through* the heart, but it has work to do throughout the system.

In the last twenty years, many of us have been sincerely working on ourselves, however inconsistently. Metaphysical tradition claims that during the last twenty-five years of every century the planet is flooded with spiritual light. We are living through the last twenty-five years not only of a century but also of a millennium.

In July 1994, a huge comet bombarded Jupiter, releasing megatons of energy more powerful than anything we've ever seen on earth. Synchronistically, this parallels the spiritual release of heretofore suppressed forces of healing and power. According to ancient astrology, Jupiter represents the higher mind, philosophy, expansion and blessing. With this bombardment in space, Jupiter's power to bless us and heal us was released and increased a millionfold.

Suddenly, in the last few years, there has been a quickening. Books that used to be the purview of only dedicated spiritual seekers now hit the bestseller lists and stay there for weeks and months. Material that used to be the cosmic gossip at ashram lunchrooms all of a sudden is on network television. As the philosopher Schopenhauer once wrote, "Every truth passes through three stages before it is recognized. In the first, it is ridiculed. In the second, it is opposed. In the third, it is regarded as self-evident."

Many still linger between ridicule and opposition, but millions of people throughout the world are beginning to regard as self-evident principles of ancient spiritual wisdom. It is not just fear that makes people curious. It is a process of "celestial speed-up" through which, although the darkness is getting darker, the light is also getting lighter. We have reached a critical mass of spiritual yearning, despite worldly appearances. There is a mass curiosity and openness to spiritual ideas, unprecedented in modern Western culture. All God needs is a crack in the door and the door is cracked. Illumination follows.

Things we thought were primitive beliefs turn out to be more sophisticated than we are. Angels arrive in a burst of light. Angels are the thoughts of God. They are the bearers of breakthrough, the mystical helmet. They deliver the mind to profound understanding.

Angels are powerful thought forms that help to hold the world together. They are the thoughts of synthesis, connection, and repair. To call on the angels is to move our attention in a higher, more creative direction, to invoke the structures of a more enlightened worldview. As our thoughts rise, the world rises. This is the resurrection of the human mind. Through its power, we can bypass a collective Armageddon. Enough of us have learned enough individually, and the world has suffered enough on every level, that should we choose, we can beam up now.

As a species, we are pregnant with a higher form of life. Pregnancy is a feminine force, and we are sourcing our new power from an ancient, more feminine energy. As we reach the end of the millennium, the Goddess makes a return to our consciousness. From appearances of the Virgin Mary to a revival of interest in Goddess religions, the feminine ascends, rising up within us, working through us as we seek a more internal power. We're not so much trying to make a place *for* ourselves *in* the world; we're trying to make a place *in* ourselves *for* the world. We are not striving to do something new, to replace external structures that no longer work. Rather we are striving to be something new, to replace internal energies that no longer work.

We cannot put new wine into old bottles. The new wine is the energy of the mystical renaissance sweeping across the planet, a psychic upheaval more profound than any political or social revolution. Efforts to strike deals with old paradigms will not meet with success. Those efforts will meet with resistance from new forces as well as old, for they will be experienced as insincere. It is too late to run back into the burning house and try to save it. It is time to build anew.

We can gain confidence in our efforts from the recognition that this renaissance is massive. The spiritual conversation in America today, and in other countries also, is the great Unsaid. It's a silent buzz. It's already here.

Just because some people don't understand it doesn't mean it isn't happening.

The mockery of those who never even took Philosophy 101, the irreverence of those whose religious experience is limited or nonexistent do not affect or slow down at all the shower of light raining down from heaven. There is a flood of spirit rising up from our ankles, permeating every cell as it goes, and in its translucent glow we are being transmuted and transported to a higher realm.

The climax of the twentieth century consists ironically in the ultimate rejection of its outstanding characteristics. With seconds to go we are remembering the Answer. We're having at last a change of heart.

Let whoever wants to laugh, laugh. No one will be laughing for too much longer. The drama is too real and the facts too incontrovertible.

The world is turning over. Something has ended. Something has begun.

· 3 ·

Mystical Power

The Lord is the Lord of all universes. This means that within every realm—material, spiritual, psychological, emotional—the same principles of creativity and materialization apply. The ways of the Lord are the processes of energy by which life moves forward. That energy is not without but within, activated as much by feeling as by thought. We move into this power through silence and communion. In the presence of God, we learn from Him His ways.

To understand the ways of the Lord is to understand the power of what is, what can be, and ultimately what shall be. Through prayer and dedication to God, we access that power in order to use it in His behalf. In that way, we co-create with God a new and better world.

All life unfolds in phases of three: First there is the realm of spirit or pure possibility. Then the arc of life moves from point to counterpoint: higher to lower, spirit to matter, love to fear, creativity to stagnation. Those two phases, however, are not the end of God's mystical blueprint. All powerlessness stems from failure to understand this point: The key to empowerment, personal and collective, is the understanding that, although darkness stalks light, the light will always reassert itself. No matter what is happening, the universe is invested in healing. Night is followed by morning. Crucifixion is followed by Resurrection. God always has the final say.

The mystical journey is a realm of devotional awareness by which we examine the meaning behind our experience and thus gain the spiritual power to endure. It is a space of greater knowing, as we transit from realms of hope, through worldly despair and ultimately on to illumination or victory. The mystical life is a life lived with an understanding of its place within the epic drama of God's unfoldment on earth. It seeks knowledge of where every situation fits into the resurrective intention of the universe. Without this understanding, we are blind and shall remain stuck in a pattern of endless repetition or sleep. Even if this is our choice, God's choice, which ultimately supersedes our own, is that we shall finally awaken. We shall be awakened by a higher emanation of mind, which is always some form of love. Our only choice is whether to awaken now or later.

This is to say that we cannot remain asleep or limited by pure materialistic consciousness forever. It is contrary to the universal order for darkness to remain. All storms pass. The prince always arrives to kiss and awaken Sleeping Beauty. The tyrants of the world, ultimately, are always defeated. So it is that the earth as we know it will yet transform into a thing of grace and beauty.

The journey of the son of God is the energetic unfoldment of all spirit and matter. That means not only that each of our lives is the son of God's journey, but that every relationship, situation, and circumstance is as well. Mystical empowerment means the strength of the mind, through understanding and awareness, to midwife the phases of death back to life, to bring down the light into regions that are darkened. The mystical keys are the keys God gives us, to cleave to Him in order to shield ourselves from the forces of abomination.

The forces of abomination are the gravitational force field pulling us away from the truth in our hearts. It is the mind of the anti-Christ, the lure of the mean thought. No earthly power has dominion over the dark one, for here within the lower heavens, his sway is as powerful as is our own. We have given him his foothold here, by constantly abdicating our responsibility to hold on to the light. Where light is let go, darkness enters. And so it is that the mind of cruelty has established its kingdom on earth.

The power to turn darkness back into the light comes not from mere human will or effort. Human strength alone is incapable of working miracles. The name of the Father, the living light, the love in our hearts, is the only conduit for spiritual victory. Spiritual victory is the only salvation. Everything else is literally wasted effort, for it shall always stray back to the beginning of itself. It lacks the power of breakthrough.

Prayer is the conduit for the reestablishment of our mental power by reclaiming its divine element. To the extent to which we think we are alone, we shall have limited power to materialize light. It is the Father's will that He share His power with us. It has been our counterwill, for some ungodly reason, to go it alone.

Thus we have been like the children of a very wealthy father, pretending to be paupers, disdaining our inheritance. But the father still wishes to pass on to us his wealth, and the world is diminished by our refusal to take our rightful place in his family. It is the natural order that the child shall receive from the father, and pass on his wealth for the good of mankind. For us to remain alone and separate from our relationship to him leaves us spiritually impoverished and without a job to do. The spiritual wealth we are to inherit is not just our gift but also our responsibility. Without that wealth, we cannot rebuild the world.

Prayer is the return of the prodigal son as we return our minds to the light from whence we came. It does not matter how long we have been gone. It does not matter the category of darkness that attracted us. It does not matter what we did while we were gone. All that matters is that we come home now, and with each of our prayers, the Father rejoices.

Mystical power stems from two basic ideas: One, do not mentally resist the darkness. Two, know that the light is coming; do not allow faithlessness to slow the process down.

To say that we will not resist darkness means that we will not fight the phases of worldly unfoldment. But we will not allow our minds to be tempted, to believe that darkness is truth. It is not truth, but very powerful illusion. God has established, within our minds, the mode of correction for our mental errors. Every religion tells the equivalent tale of how the Father does not leave us to destroy ourselves. He has sent Himself forth to us. He brings us home.

The righteous mind becomes a tool for the rebuilding of the earthly kingdom. The mind that has been graced with light becomes the vessel of the world's illumination. The purpose of prayer is the alignment of the mind with the thoughts and the will of God.

The world as we know it is a realm of trapped light, light that we must release back to the forces of healing and correction. The key to this release is conscious attention, which is what prayer is. When faced with pain, we are tempted to look the other way. The key to victory is to look it straight in the eye.

We don't go to God as a way to ignore our pain. We go there to give Him our pain, that we might soften around it as we relax into our trust in Him. We then become bigger than the pain, and thus able to absorb it. As we surrender our despair to the process of God's alchemical action within us, the pain moves through us more quickly. Our illumination moves it out.

At every moment, we are somewhere along the road of the journey of the son of God. The key to mystical power lies in understanding and accepting our place in the journey at a particular time.

If you're at the beginning of something and everything's great, then by all means be happy, but do not take things for granted. If you're experiencing the meanness or betrayal of the world, then by all means be sad, but know that you are not defeated. If you are in the midst of your resurrection and rebirth, then do not forget to praise and give thanks. As mystics, we are aware of the phases of the journey, that the phases might flow more perfectly through our lives.

As the Jews were led out of Egypt and saved from the Pharaoh's evil power, *even when it meant that the sea would have to part;* as Jesus resurrected, *even when it meant that physical death would have to turn into life,* so it is that God's victory is not limited by the laws of time and space as we understand them. This is the essential building block of our quantum burst out of spiritual darkness: God's power is the power to reverse all physical laws. By ourselves, of course, we are without this power. Through His power within us, we are workers of miracles and the seedlings of a transformed humanity.

We shall become as different from who we are now as the butterfly is different from the caterpillar. The great religious entities are examples of illumination, for they are fully actualized children of God. They have claimed His spirit and thus become the materialization of enlightenment.

As we worship the masters, we grasp their journey, their transformation from mortal to immortal beings. Their beingness is our destiny, and their having achieved what they have gives them the power to help us achieve the same. What we seek to achieve is the enlightened mind, the illumined attitudes of acceptance and release, the ultimate conviction and capacity to cast out fear through our ability to love. Our radical forgiveness, our faith in love's power, runs counter to the ways of the world. The masters are ones who refashion the world by having been themselves refashioned.

Our commitment to being part of humanity's rebirth is our commitment to fundamental change. The change we seek cannot be achieved through any human auspices, but only through the spirit of God. Waiting outside an embattled town are the reinforcements we need in order to win this war, the endless battles we keep waging against the lower energies within ourselves. We must invite the light into us and restore the bridges, open the gates by which it might enter our lives. Spiritual practice is the opening of the gates, now all but locked against God's love.

What is our resistance? What has God done to us that we should reject Him so entirely? What has been His crime that we do not allow the all-empowering force of the universe to help us or even give us comfort? Each of us answers this question for ourselves, as we examine why we avoid the use of the eagle's wings that have been given to us, yet struggle so hard to get the sparrow to lend us his.

And we all know the answer: We were taught such lies as children, lies about God's anger, His revenge and His judgment. We were taught such irrelevant historical tales instead of being shown the blinding light, more dazzling than a thousand suns, that is the truth of God's love passed on from heart to heart. We see such bastardization of His teachings all around us, more small-minded than enlightening, more controlling than liberating, posing as His arbiters yet clearly His obstructers. Shall we be so stupid as to think there is no light in that package, some illumined force that must be awesome indeed for so much power to be marshalled against our seeing it? If darkness comes out in direct response and with concomitant strength to the light, then given the evils of the history of institutionalized religion, how beautiful the Lord must be.

God is more than capable of direct contact with each of us, as we are capable of direct contact with Him. Each of us has equal capacity for divine insight. We need only lean to Him. In time we give, in devotion we show, in efforts to love and serve and forgive each other, we partake of the spiritual connection that restores the link between the Father and His separated children.

Just as the founding of democracy relocated the center of political power from the king to the individual, so shall the spiritual revolution of our times relocate the center of true religious power, in truth as well as fiction, from religious institutions to the heart of the human being. That is where it used to be. That is where it belongs.

There is nowhere you need go to find God, for God is within you. There is no one you need ask if you are good enough, for He has already established He is exceedingly well pleased. There is no one you need look to for victory, except the One who has risen within you. As He rose, He took all of us with Him. His resurrection has been established; we need not seek it, but rather claim it as our own, as we face the crucifixions of a cruel and bitter world. Through Him we hold the keys to triumph and transcendence. It doesn't matter what religion we are. It doesn't matter what doctrine we ascribe to. It doesn't matter what people say. What matters is that we open our inner eyes, and see the beauty of the risen

One in every heart and every leaf. The Christ is not a Christian concept. The Christ is a force of nature, *our* nature. It no more belongs to a particular group than the ocean belongs to Greenpeace.

How beautiful the world will be when we have mystically journeyed back up to the light. When all lower thought has been transformed into its highest possibility, when all human energies have been freed from the tyranny of fear, how light we will be, how released we will feel. And the time is now: We can accept the future in the present moment. The Jews say the Messiah is coming; the Christians say the Messiah has been here; Einstein said that there is no time. The truth is, the Messiah is within. It doesn't matter what we call it or how we frame it. All that matters is that we claim our inheritance, the power of God to heal and redeem us. Forget the language. Just build a new world.

The church or any true religious congregation is a mystical phenomenon, a gathering of souls in a collective search for God's presence. It has little to do with outer form; it has everything to do with the purity of our hearts. Spiritual fellowship is on the rise again, as we return to a conscious awareness of its significance. Where two or more are gathered in God, His light within us accelerates and intensifies. Nothing is more powerful than an agreement between two people. The more a thought is shared, the stronger it becomes. So it is that we are recognizing anew the power we have to heal the world, as we join with each other in worship and prayer.

The path of healing is the path of the pilgrim. Many of us became seekers over the last several years as we began to read the literature of sacred philosophical journeys. Then, as we continued our search and deepened our commitment, something else began to happen. To be a seeker still implies that there is a road to be found. After several years of searching, many people find their roads: some kind of spiritual path. At a certain point, the seeker becomes a pilgrim. We are no longer looking for the road; we are *on* the road. We are walking it, surrounded by other pilgrims. Sometimes we walk fast; sometimes we walk slow. Some people are further ahead; some people lag behind. Sometimes it's a pleasant walk; sometimes the road is treacherous and our knees are bloody. But we know we are on the right road and that others have reached its end. Those who did found God there, and in so doing they illumined the world.

The pilgrimage is a process by which we change what we think and transform who we are. Prayer is the pilgrim's walking stick. We pray for the capacity to forgive, to see the innocence in people and to surrender all things to God. We pray to enter the mystery, to remember now, to no longer forget.

The highest level of prayer is not a prayer *for* anything. It is a deep and profound silence, in which we allow ourselves to be still and know Him. In that silence, we are changed. We are calmed. We are illumined. Prayer is meant to dissolve the worldly focus, to dissolve our sense of a separate self, to help us detach from an insane world order. We pray that He might flood our minds. Prayer is like pouring hot water on an ice cube, melting the cold and encrusted thought forms that still surround our hearts.

It is worth great effort. When we wake up in the morning, it's a good idea *not* to go directly to newspaper, radio, television or coffee. Those things testify to the reality of the outer world. By the act of our perceiving that world, we fortify our attachment to it. The outer world is the realm of the nonessential. To the extent that we focus on it, we remain stuck in the realm of effect and not cause.

The inner world is the realm of the essential, in the world and in ourselves. The realm of the essential is the realm of the artist, the philosopher, the holy, the pure. By the act of our perceiving it, we fortify our experience of it. It is the realm not of effect, but of cause. It is the purpose of our lives to cause a better world.

If the first thing we do each morning is to concentrate on the realm of effect, then for the rest of the day we shall be at effect, of thoughts, feelings and circumstances over which we seem to have no control. The newspaper will not reveal God's truth to us, nor will television news. We can scan them forever, but they will not turn us toward ourselves. That is not their function. They exist to report on the outer world, and to the extent to which we base our experience of life on what they tell us, we will be at the effect of the lies of the world. Just say no to psychic death. No, I will not read the papers in the morning before I've read something inspirational. No, I will not watch TV before I meditate. No, I will not drink caffeine before I have consciously shown love or prayed for someone.

The search for God is a lifestyle decision. Fill your mind with the meaningless stimuli of a world preoccupied with meaningless things, and it will not be easy to feel peace in your heart. Fill your mind with the things of God, and peace will flow into you like water into the ground.

We want more than talk, more than words. Yet prayer is talk and words that break through the constrictions normally associated with both. Prayer has intercessionary power to enter into the consciousness of normal life and expand its possibilities.

I've heard it said that prayer is when we talk to God, and meditation is when we listen. Meditation is a time of quiet when the mind is freed from its attachment to the hysterical ravings of a world gone mad. It is a silence in which the spirit of God can enter us and work His divine alchemy upon us. Our brains literally emit different brain waves as we receive information more deeply than we do during normal waking consciousness. There are many forms of meditation, and when we ask in our hearts for God to reveal our path to us, the mystical process of the inner teachings begins to unfold to our conscious mind. There is Jewish meditation, Christian meditation, transcendental meditation, Buddhist meditation, the workbook of *A Course in Miracles* and many more paths. What matters is not the path; what matters is its destination. All genuine spiritual teachings lead us back to the reality of God.

Nothing is more important to the future of the world than that millions of people begin daily, prolonged meditation and prayer. Why is meditation and prayer our greatest hope for world salvation, the vehicle for our spiritual renaissance? Because it transforms us at the level of cause. Prayer is a conduit for miracles. It addresses the problems of the world at their source. It changes people at a cellular level, and with each one who changes, others are brought miraculously closer to enlightenment.

The priest or priestess, rabbi or minister, therapist or healer is a brother or sister who facilitates the journey. It is the job of spiritual companionship to verbalize and hold in consciousness the principles of spiritual truth, that the pilgrim might walk the path more easily. Spiritual practice uplifts a society because it counters the thought forms of selfishness and greed. It purifies the air, cleansing the environment of mental and emotional toxins, the pollutants that actually threaten us most. People who still exploit each other cannot be expected to stop exploiting nature. The environmental cleanup most necessary to save us is a cleanup of all the filth in our minds.

Spiritual work is not easy. It means the willingness to surrender feelings that seem, while we're in them, like our defense against a greater pain. It means we surrender to God our perceptions of all things.

Spiritual values present a radical alternative to the world's prevailing thought system.

We are renewed and cleansed as we receive the pure and vibrant energy transmissions being sent by God to heal us. This is the purpose of meditation and prayer, that we might open to receive His programs of redemption and resurrection. His love, sent down from the highest levels, can penetrate the veils of worldly error. It changes our coding as planetary beings, imprinting us with God's plans for our salvation and rebirth. We are graduating to a new level of awareness, and with it shall come a new sense of oneness with each other and with God. We can, through continued and sincere devotional practice, transmute the world of material form. We shall bring it into harmony with the structures of the living light. We shall live from that light and become that light. What lies before us will one day be known as a Great Transformation of the human race.

If we choose to remain with meaningless thoughts, preoccupied with meaningless things, then we will continue to experience meaningless patterns of existence. This will not change our coding or our potential, however. We have the choice, at every moment, to leave the world of death behind us and enter, through prayerfulness, the gates of heaven. There *is* a gate. It is not illusion or metaphor, but rather an energetic force field in which the thoughts of fear are transformed to love, the darkest nights illumined by dawn.

God issues forth His directives for resurrection in any situation, at any time or place.

Miraculous power is bound by nothing. There is no pattern of darkness beyond God's mercy, which is to say that His forgiveness and power are total. Let us go to Him. The world as we know it is out of sync with the vibrations of the name of the Father; as we invoke His name, we bring the world back into His arms. There, the bonds of darkness are loosened, the chains that bind us are broken, the walls that separate us are melted. Our shared faith in His power is our mental agreement that He can do what we cannot do to repair our lives and bring us out of the lower worlds.

Still it is not enough to believe in God's power; we must wish to serve it, to elongate the light. We must give our lives to Him, that He might use us in His work. Thus we become who we have not been and ascend to higher realms, beyond our current three-dimensional limitations. We are like houses that have not had the lights turned on yet. We keep adding furniture, but still the rooms are dark. We have scarcely seen the light that awaits us.

Something huge is happening. There has never been a time more fertile for the preparation of mass ascension. We are initiates, however un-likely, into the great and higher mysteries. All of us. The light pops up where you least expect it. God, like every brilliant force, appreciates irony and the dance of the nonobvious.

Whoever we are and wherever we've been, there is a blueprint for our miraculous rebirth. All of the areas of darkness in our lives, individually and collectively, can still be returned to eternal unfoldment. Prayer is our refocusing of the energies of the world.

We have been so long in a downward spin. The angels now offer us an antigravitation option. We are meant to fly and with our spirits we can. We are meant to ascend, to transmute the negative mass of the world's corrupted thought forms. No one asked us to stay so long, away from heaven, away from joy.

We needn't wait. We can go home now.

PART TWO

PRAYERS

*"Make every effort to pray from the
heart. Even if you do not succeed,
in the eyes of the Lord the
effort is precious."*

from The Gates of Prayer:
The New Union Jewish Prayer Book

Ladders to God

Prayer reweaves the rent fabric of the universe. It releases us, in time, from the snares of lower energies. Total dependence on God makes us independent of the darkness of the world. No problem is too big or small, no question too important or unimportant to place in His hands. We don't ask God for too much; in fact, we ask Him for far too little. Turn to Him for everything. Give everything to God. The mistake many people make is that although they *believe* in Him, they do not intimately include Him in their lives.

Prayer and meditation reconnect us with our Source. We have gradually become so disassociated from nature, including our own inner

nature, that we tend to perceive ourselves as separate from our own ground of being. Spirit is the
essence of who we are, the divine energy that per-
meates all life. To defer to God, to appeal to Him
is to humble our mortal, limited selves before the
force of consciousness at the center of all things.

And so we embark upon the ways of a prayerful life. Prayer is where we talk to God, stake
claim to His thought forms and honor His
power to heal us. Prayerful ways are not always
easy, for our resistance is great. We have been
deluded by the thinking of an arrogant world.
Prayer roots us in a different center of emotional
gravity. It represents a true conversion from
sourcing power in one place to sourcing it in
another. It is the spiritualization of our mental
habits and the disciplining of our scattered
minds. That is why it gives us so much strength.

Prayers increases our faith in the power of
good and thus our power to invoke it. Most of us
have more faith in the power of AIDS to kill us
than we have faith in God to heal us and make
us whole. We have more faith in the power of
violence to destroy us than we have faith in the
power of love to restore us. Where we place our

faith, there we will find our treasure. Whatever we choose to look at, we will see. Prayer is a way of focusing our eyes.

Our goal is to bring our lives to prayer. Emotionally, there are no small issues. Anything has the power to hurt, if our mind is vicious enough to use it against us. A torn shirt can drive us to tears, if it reminds us enough of a day in third grade when we felt like our clothes weren't adequate. A small, careless word from someone can trigger a torrent of painful feelings. It, is these small, insidious moments of pain that God can cast out but that we alone cannot. Hurt children, their wounds unhealed, too often become very dangerous adults.

We spiritually reconstitute our lives by asking Him to enter us. We ask Him into every situation, to alchemize our thoughts and emotions, to change dramatically our orientation. The ways of prayerfulness are a modulation up from a mode of despair to a mode of hope. A desperate outlook is a choice we make. Peace is simply another one.

Our prayer is for our hearts to stretch to the point of total openness, to radical acceptance and love of others. The path of the pilgrim is the path to a heart that expands and does not constrict. That doesn't mean we won't have sorrowful days, but if there is sorrow, we want sorrow that matters. Both sorrow and joy can stretch us and hone us. The issue is not whether our day is easy, but whether we spend it with an open heart. We use prayer to redesign our lives. We use it to get our minds, and therefore our lives, back on track. After that, we use it to stay there.

"Dear God, please handle this or that" is a prayer for perfection. It means, Please infuse my contribution to this situation with Your wisdom and Your power. Shed Your light. If there is a lack of perfect unfoldment here, I want whatever blocks in my mind contribute to this problem to be revealed to me and removed. Deliver all darkness to the nothingness from whence it came.

With this attitudinal shift, we change the paradigm that now rules the world. Just as we used to think that the earth was the center of external power and then found out that the sun is, we have been thinking that man's ego is the center of internal power and, at last, we're remembering that God is.

Of course this is blasphemy to the ego; it robs it of its power. But the ego has never given us anything but the illusion of power in our lives. Our choice is to be slaves to the ego, or actualized children of God. God shares His power with us to the extent to which we acknowledge Him as Source. That is not because *He* has an ego, by the way; it is because without that conscious acknowledgement the subconscious mind remains confused about which master it is supposed to serve. Prayer programs divine guidance into the mental computer. It is not an abdication of personal responsibility but rather a profound *taking* of responsibility, the ultimate step toward our full divine empowerment on earth.

Ancient wisdom, then, is modern wisdom.

Humanity's fall from grace means humanity's predilection for thinking the meanest, most fearful, least loving thoughts. The thoughts of God are the thoughts of the Most High, while the thoughts of the fallen human race are thoughts most low. Paradise is the realm of higher thought, and prayer is our ladder back up there.

Prayer is something we *do*. To say a prayer is more than just to think about God. A prayerful attitude is powerful, but the actual utterance of a prayer, silently or aloud, increases the subconscious power of communion with God. In this sense, prayer is God's greatest gift to us, for it is the key to His house.

I once read in an essay on Buddhism that "nothing is so fragile as action without prayer." Prayer aligns our internal energies with truth in a way that mere action cannot. Events ultimately unfold according to subconscious rather than conscious programming, and prayer is a way of healing and releasing the subconscious mind. When we pray that God take a situation into His hands, we are praying for two things: one, that events unfold at the highest vibration of love for all human beings touched in any way by a situation, now and forever; and two, that our minds remain aligned with truth.

If things go well, we pray that we not be tempted to get cocky, proud, or to take success for granted. If things do not go well, we pray that we not be tempted to think the jury is ever in until we see God smiling. It is only giving in to defeat that ultimately brings defeat. Initial rejection or disappointment does not mean that

God is saying no. It means we're being given the opportunity to see past a crucifixion and to attitudinally invoke resurrection. Prayer gives us the strength to endure, the tools to make miracles.

A few years ago, I was visiting my friend Rose, who found that her daughter was not at a friend's home, where we thought she was. Upon further investigation, we found that not only was she not there, but in fact none of her friends had seen her since ten o'clock the night before. As Rose called every place she could think of to locate her daughter, her panic understandably began to mount. I tried to be helpful but as the list of possibilities narrowed, I too became scared for her daughter's safety. Rose took a Valium to help her relax.

After about twenty minutes, when no further options presented themselves, I said, "Let's say a prayer." We did. Soon after, Rose looked up at me, a deep serenity on her face, and said, "Oh, good, the Valium just kicked in." As the irony of what she had just said dawned on her, we burst into our first big laugh of the day. Then her daughter called, safe and sound. Boy, is Valium powerful . . .

My friend was delivered from hell not by the power of drugs but by the power of heaven. The interrelationship between the two states is the meaning of our existence. The physical symbols of both Judaism and Christianity—the Star of David and the cross—represent the right relationship between Heaven and earth, the axis of God meeting the axis of humanity: As it is above, so shall it be below. To look to God means to look to the realm of consciousness that can deliver us from the pain of living.

The purpose of prayer is to bring Heaven and earth together. It gives inner peace in ways that neither intellectual understanding, credentials, money, sex, drugs, houses, clothes, nor any other gifts of the world can do. We can learn to speak to God as we would speak to a combination therapist/ lover/teacher/best friend/One-we-trust-more-than-anything/One-who-loves-us-no-matter-what/ One-with-all-the-power-to-heal/One-with-the-power-and-desire-to-help, for that's what God is. Prayer work is a constant and consistent conversation with Him. God listens, and He answers. His answer is always peace.

Prayer gives us access to a sweeter, more abundant life. The intellect gives many things, but ultimately it cannot give comfort. No conventional therapy can release us from a deep and abiding psychic pain. Through prayer we find what we cannot find elsewhere: a peace that is not of this world.

· 2 ·

Daily Prayers

DAILY RENEWAL:
PRAYER AND MEDITATION

E ach morning, or any time you are about to
go anywhere or do anything, go over the sce-
nario in your mind. Pray, consciously, that the
circumstance in question be used for the purposes of love, that God's rays of light might
shine upon it.

Part of our mind is bent on love, and part of
it is bent on fear. That is how consciousness
operates. The loving mind is called the spirit of
God, the Holy Spirit, the *Shechina,* and many
other names. It is the holy Self that lies potential
within all of us, the mystical drive to return
home. We always have the choice to align our-

selves with its presence and act accordingly in the world or give in to fear and, on some level, die.

The problem is that the voice of the spirit is not the dominant voice of the world. Fear is louder than love here. It takes conscious effort, therefore, to go against the voices of the world and to actualize our spiritual nature.

The fearful mind, or the negative ego, is alive and well within us and around us, but darkness disappears in the presence of light. Fear has no ultimate power in a situation dedicated through prayer to God.

The purpose of daily prayer is the cultivation of a sense of the sacred. Sacred energy renews us. Lives with no more sense of spiritual meaning than that provided by shopping malls, ordinary television, and stagnant workplaces are barren lives indeed. Spirituality enriches culture. Prayer enables us to transform the world, because it transforms us. From the moment we awaken each morning, our minds are at work in one direction or the other. Either we are slaves to the fearful mental habit patterns that dominate our world, or we are consciously taking part in the counter-force to the world's despair.

We embark upon the creation of a peaceful lifestyle by recognizing the need, daily, to cleanse our minds just as we cleanse our bodies. Through morning prayers and meditation, we embark upon the day spiritually prepared. Without this preparation, we enter the day with yesterday's anxieties— our own and those of millions of others. Through the grace of God, we can be cleansed each day of yesterday's sorrow and yesterday's pain.

The more we allow our internal world to be illumined, the more our external world will take on meaning. Through meditation and prayer, our nervous systems become prepared for the task of a more powerful external existence. People who love will usher in the new, illumined world. As we turn Godward, the energies of true life stream into our minds and through our hearts. To go within is not to turn our backs on the world; it is to prepare ourselves to serve it most effectively.

What we need: a comfortable, private place; silence, or as close to it as we can get; and a commitment to making spiritual practice a part of our lives. We must spend as much time as we feel we can give each morning to the communion with God that will expand our consciousness, renew our spirit, and guide our thoughts throughout the day. Silent contemplation, or meditation, is as important a factor in spiritual transformation as is prayer. Along with reading spiritual literature, prayer and meditation form the backbone of our daily practice. Almost any meditation technique we choose takes twenty minutes, at least. Prayer doesn't take long, but the effect it has is miraculous.

Read my prayers or someone else's. By all means, create your own. It can be very powerful to write down prayers. Some people find value in keeping a prayer journal. These principles, in general, are good to remember:

- Invite God's spirit into every situation, which means to ask for the highest level of thought, guidance, and unfoldment to occur for all concerned.
- Ask God to remove from your mind all thoughts that are not of Him.
- Ask God to show you the love and innocence within all people.
- Ask that only God's purposes be served in every situation.
- Be honest. Be humble. Be serious.

MORNING PRAYER

Dear God,
I give this day to You.
May my mind stay centered on the things of
    spirit.
May I not be tempted to stray from love.
As I begin this day, I open to receive You.
Please enter where You already abide.
May my mind and heart be pure and true,
    and may I not deviate from the things of
    goodness.
May I see the love and innocence in all
    mankind, behind the masks we all wear and
    the illusions of this worldly plane.
I surrender to You my doings this day.
I ask only that they serve You and the healing of
    the world.
May I bring Your love and goodness with me, to
    give unto others wherever I go.
Make me the person You would have me be.
Direct my footsteps, and show me what You
    would have me do.
Make the world a safer, more beautiful place.
Bless all Your creatures.

Heal us all, and use me, dear Lord, that I might
  know the joy of being used by You.
Amen.

A NEW DAY

Dear God,
Thank you for this new day, its beauty and its
  light.
Thank You for my chance to begin again.
Free me from the limitations of yesterday.
Today may I be reborn.
May I become more fully a reflection of Your
  radiance.
Give me strength and compassion and courage
  and wisdom.
Show me the light in myself and others.
May I recognize the good that is available every-
  where.
May I be, this day, an instrument of love and
  healing.
Lead me into gentle pastures.
Give me deep peace that I might serve You most
  deeply.
Amen.

❦

Our daily prayer work creates a context for the transformation of who we are and what we do. Every morning, we ask to be made new. Every evening, we take stock of how well we did this day—where we rose up in glory, and where we stumbled and fell.

It's very powerful to go over the events of our day, mentally, as honestly as we can. God is not our judge but our Healer. If there is someone we are holding grievances toward, a prayer of forgiveness is vital. If we can see an area where we ourselves did not fulfill our most noble potential, let us pray for correction and miraculous transformation. What can we consciously give thanks for? What things were wonderful, in others, in ourselves? Where did we slip—snap at someone, fail to forgive or act out of integrity?

An example of an evening's conversation with God:

Dear God,

When my mother called today, I was very rude. I was so impatient with her, with her meaningless questions. She has started to forget things, and it is so mean of me, the way I snap at her and make her feel stupid. I want to get over this, God. I want to outgrow the immature way I react to her and rebel against her. Please help me. Please change me. Please open my heart and make me into the daughter You would have me be.

Amen.

Or:

Dear God,

When I talked to Michael today, I was very harsh with him. I'm still so unforgiving of the things that happened last month, and I know that if I can't forgive him, we'll stay stuck in this conflict. My anger is hurting me more than it's hurting him. Please help me see him as he exists now. Please help me stop focusing on his mistakes, and help me see his innocence. Show me his good, and teach me how to support and respect him most effectively. Make me a blessing in his life.

Amen.

EVENING PRAYERS

Dear God,

Thank You for this day.

Thank You for my safety and the safety of my
loved ones.

As I enter sleep, may these hours give me peace.

May they bring healing to my mind and body.

While I sleep, dear Lord, please bless the world.

Where there is pain, where there are people who
have no place to sleep, who suffer and who
die, may Your angels come unto them and
minister to their hearts.

Dear Lord,

Please let the light stream in.

Please use my hours of sleep.

Please prepare me, during these hours of rest,
for greater service to You.

May the light that surrounds me, tomorrow
shine through me.

Soften my heart.

Thank You, Lord.

Amen.

Dear God,

I surrender to You the day now over.

May only the love remain.

Take all else into the fire of Your transformative
power.

Release me, release others, from any effects of
my wrongmindedness.

As I now give to You who I am, what I did, who
I loved, who I failed to love, please make all
things right.

Take all things.

May I continue to grow in Your light and love.

Tomorrow, may I be better.

Amen.

3

Prayers for the Soul

PRAYERS FOR NEW LIFE

Dear God,

Be my redeemer, my internal teacher, my divine
    physician.

Thank You for Your presence in my life.

I surrender to You all I am, all I think, all I feel,
    and all I have.

I recognize in this moment that Yours is the
    power to heal and make whole.

You who have the power to work miracles, You
    who rule time and space, please take me in
    Your arms and hold me.

Dear Lord, please lift me up and heal me.

Cast out of my mind all thoughts that are not
    of You.

Cast out of me all harsh and critical nature.
Cast out of me all violence and all anger.
Cast out of me all demons from my past.
For I would be made new.
I wish to walk so close to You that we might be
    as one.
I ask for new life, new mind, new body, new spirit.
Dear God, please come into me and release me
    from this pain.
Amen.

Dear God,
Today, this day, I give to You.
Do within me what You want to do.
Please make of my heart Your vessel and servant.
May the glorious light of the Lord of Creation
    find a restful home inside my soul.
May I be no more who I used to be.
I now embrace the divine child within me.
May it burst forth now to bless the world.
May I not be tempted to doubt the light that
    lights the entire world.
Illumine the earth and save the world.
Thank You, Lord.
Amen.

〜✦〜

Dear God,

On this day I ask for new life.

I ask to be reborn in spirit and mind.

I choose to consider as possible, through the
grace of God, the total transformation of my
mind and body.

The mystical nature of who I really am is
known to You, dear God, but not to me.

Let me see revealed the depth and power of my
true Self.

Amen.

〜✦〜

Dear God,

May I be pregnant with the expression of a new
being: someone more magnificent than I have
ever been;

More powerful than I have ever been;

Healthier than I have ever been;

More alive than I have ever been;

More at cause than I have ever been;

More tender than I have ever been;
More compassionate and merciful than I have
    ever been;
More full of love than I have ever been;
More tolerant, less judgmental than I have ever
    been;
More at one with myself and all others;
More close to You, dear Lord, than I have ever
    been.
Amen.

~e~

Dear God,
I now take one step further to absolute and
    total reliance on You.
Let me not be tempted to deviate.
Let me not be tempted to look elsewhere for
    final answers, but rather may the power of
Your spirit burst forth into my life.
Come one step further to me as I have come to
    You.
Amen.

For almost every worldly source of happiness, there is a fear-based reason to worry. We may have incredible children, for instance, but a day doesn't go by that we're not concerned about their welfare for one reason or another. The very fact that we love our children so much, juxtaposed with all the danger in the world, is enough to keep any parent anxious. We may have a great career, but the pressures are intense. We may have wonderful relationships, but people are still people. We may have a lovely home but there are big responsibilities to that one, too.

Children are happy because they don't yet have a file in their minds called "All the Things That Could Go Wrong." They don't have a mind-set that puts "Things to Fear" before "Things to Love." Unless we can be like little children, we can't enter into the kingdom of heaven; unless we can be like little children, we can't be happy. Children are happy because they don't have all the facts yet.

Facts are what we must completely let go of if we want to be happy. We must *decide* to fly above the turmoil if we really want to fly above it. We must ignore, maturely not immaturely, a whole realm of so-called meaning. As long as our self-identification centers around what we call the real world, no profound happiness is possible. Happiness requires that we give up a worldly orientation—not worldly *things* but a worldly *attachment* to things. We have to surrender all outcomes. We have to live here but appreciate the joke.

In order to be happy, we must become bigger than the worldly self. It's a phenomenal challenge to do that, because the world does not support our expansion into superbeings. Just as children play games in which they pretend to be adults, and thus pave the way for adulthood, so you and I must pretend to be angelic, noble, enlightened spirits just visiting here, in order to actually become them.

This planet is being peopled by superior creatures who are going to save us, but they aren't arriving from the outside; they're arriving from the inside. They're bleeping in and out. They're our future selves coming back to pick us up, in order that there might *be* a future. We're being beckoned by fellows up ahead on the road, and as we look at them, our walk to where they are goes faster. That's how religious worship works: It collapses the time it takes to reach the spiritual vicinity of who and what we worship.

❧

Dear God,

Please make me a force for Good.

Remove from my awareness all thoughts that keep me bound here.

Every goal I surrender to You.

All agendas I surrender to You.

All I have and all I am I give to You.

I ask only to be carried in Your arms that I might know the joy of full surrender.

May I not be tempted to think about meaningless things and give them weight and suffer thereby.

Please send Your spirit to lift me up, above the pain and turmoil of this world.

Please give me new youth, and a free and joyful spirit.

Show me the happiness of full forgiveness.

Whomever I do not forgive, dear Lord, please
  show me how, for I wish to be free of the
  guilt of this world.

Dear God,

Please make me happy.

I am ready to outgrow my childish pain.

Amen.

PRAYERS FOR DEPRESSION

Dear God,

I feel such pain, anxiety and depression.

I know this is not Your will for me, and yet my
  mind is held in chains by fear and paranoia.

I surrender my life, right now, to You.

Take the entire mess, all of it, now too compli-
  cated to explain to anyone but known by You
  in each detail.

Do what I cannot do.

Lift me up.

Give me a new chance.

Show me a new light.

Make me a new person.

Dear God,

This depression frightens me.
Dear God,
Please bring me peace.
Amen.

⌘

Dear God,
The pain of this life is more than I can bear.
I feel as though death would be better.
My thoughts are dark, my sorrows huge.
I feel as though I shall not endure, and there is
    no one and nothing to turn to now.
My hurt is so big.
I cannot handle this.
If You can, dear God, please do.
If You can, please do.
Amen.

PRAYER FOR THE HIGHER SELF

Dear God,
In this one moment I recognize that there is
    within me a perfect Self:
A Self that is not dysfunctional;

A Self that is not weak but strong;

That is not limited, but unlimited;

That is not small, but huge;

That is not in pain but in peace;

That is not faithless and scared but all-knowing, all loving, and serene and calm, through the grace of God.

I have been playing with the toys of death and weakness.

I have been playing at sickness and playing at addiction.

I have been playing at dysfunction and limitation and war.

I have been playing at hunger and violation of myself and others.

I have been playing with toys that are dangerous.

But I desire to play the games of death no more.

In this moment, I ask You, dear God, to release me from my destructive thinking.

I take up now the mantle of Your magnificence.

Through Your grace, dear God, I am good and innocent and strong and pure, for thus would You have me be.

The love that emanates from Your mind to me, and from my mind to the minds of others, is a power so great. Within its embrace all nega-

tivity shall turn to good, all pain to peace, all
fear to love.

I invoke Your light.

I receive Your heaven, which replaces hell.

I do not look back.

I do not stop my eyes at the veil of horror that
surrounds the world, but rather I extend my
vision to the possibilities for love for myself
and others.

I step out of my childhood, into my adulthood;
out of my weaknesses, into my strengths; out
of my fear, into my love, out of my small
self, into You.

Dear God, please make me new.

Amen.

CLEARING UP THE PAST

We have all made mistakes. We have all done
things that we wish we had not done. We have all
missed opportunities and blown more of them
than we care to admit.

But the universe begins a new cycle whenever
we are ready. God is willing to start again when
we are. In His eyes, we are like newborn children,

and at any given moment we can be reborn. As we atone for our errors, we are released from their effects.

See the light, and your life will reflect it. Deny the light, and in your blindness you will create chaos. When you choose to open your eyes again, the chaos shall be no more.

⸎

Dear God,
The burden that I carry feels too big for me.
I'm so scared that this situation is going to fall
    apart and blow up in my face.
I have done the following things that I regret:
    (*say your own*).
I failed to do the following things that I feel I
    should have done: (*say your own*).
And now, dear Lord, I feel so guilty.
The situation is out of control, and I am so
    scared.
Please God, I need a miracle.
Please give me the chance to begin again.
I give to You what I tried to keep under my own
    control before, and now everything has gone
    wrong, of course.

Dear Lord, I am so sorry.

Please help me now,

May I begin again.

I place this entire situation in Your hands.

May it be reborn.

Please forgive me my errors and help me to forgive others for theirs.

Do for me what I cannot do for myself.

I go back in my mind to the moment at which I
went astray in my thinking.

I surrender all aspects of this event to You.

From this point forward, I will not feel guilty,
for I know You will make right what I have
made wrong.

Thank You, Lord, for Your power and Your
willingness to use it on my behalf.

I pray that I might learn to do wrong no longer,
that I might be a better person in the future.

Thank You for the chance to begin again.

Amen.

Dear God,

Please take my past and take my future.

Transform them both through the miracle of
Your power into energies of love and love
only.

May I know the present as You would have me
see it.

May I see only You in everyone and everything
that I might be dazzled by the light, lifted up
by the light, given joy by the light, and made
new by the light.

Release me from my past and deliver me to my
future.

In You I trust; nothing else is real.

In You I have faith; nothing else has power.

And so it is that I am where I belong, and I
shall strive for nothing.

I am at home; may I feel this and be at peace.

For I would rob myself no longer through my
vain imaginings and tormented thoughts.

You are my life.

You are here and now.

Amen.

Most of us agree that a breakdown of personal responsibility has led to a general breakdown of social order. While we are tempted at times to think that other people are the problem, our most adult response to the problems of the world is to take full responsibility for our own part in them.

The cleanup work begins at home. Ask God to remove your character defects. Get as specific as you can. Use this prayer to completely open up to a divine love and healing in your heart. No one but God is listening. No one is judging you. God does not desire to punish, but to heal you. You are punished only by yourself, to the extent that you keep your darkness hidden. Reveal it to God. Ask the Lord to heal you. Miracles will happen.

Spending hours and hours trying to figure out how we got so messed up is ultimately not as powerful as surrendering our character defects to God and asking Him to take them away.

In the silence of meditation, God's spirit has a chance to enter us, to do a sort of psychic surgery upon us, to rewire our souls at the deepest levels.

The value of the Catholic confession, the Jewish Day of Atonement, or the "personal moral inventory" of Alcoholics Anonymous lies in the way we bring unconscious darkness into the light. Instead of trying to hide our faults, we consciously aim to find them in order to deliver them into the hands of God. God will take from us only the things we release to Him. We don't have to hide from God's vengeance, for God is not vengeful.

When we do show up in conscious awareness of our weaknesses, it's important that we hold to the faith in God's power to heal us. Sometimes we think we're so messed up that only several more years of therapy or recovery work could possibly rid us of all these faults. But this is not an attitude of true power; it is arrogance masquerading as spiritual modesty, because it doubts the power of God to heal us. We must modulate from the purely psychological to the mystical, and claim the radical healing possibilities of grace.

When does God heal us? Right here, right now. It might seem to take time, for the healing might unfold in time, but healing is given in the instant we request it. God's answer is as clear as our willingness to hear it. God's healing is always some form of wisdom.

To appeal to God is to appeal to the action of universal love. Love never fails to come when we call to it, but it will always seem to fail us when our bidding is self-centered. The most powerful prayers are simply for God's will to be done, because God's will is healing for all living things.

⤞⤝

Dear God,
I want so much to be the person You would
    have me be.
There are so many places in my life where I still
    hide from You, where I deny my love.
In this moment I surrender those places to You.
Please heal me, Lord.
I know that I:

· make it hard for other people to get close
    to me
· withhold my forgiveness
· hold prejudices against certain people
· am mean to some people

- gossip
- lie
- cheat
- play small
- steal or violate
- manipulate
- hold resentments
- take people and situations for granted
- (*say your own*)

Turn my darkness, dear Lord, into Light.
May I become Your Self within me.
Illumine my heart.
Increase my understanding.
May my footsteps go where You would have
    them go, and my actions be what You would
    have them be.
Dear Lord, please make me new.
Amen.

Dear God,
Remove from me my darkness.
Reveal to me Your light, which You share with
    me and have placed within me.
May I shine forth as Your beloved child.

May Your spirit cleanse my heart and mind.
May I feel forgiven.
Please set me free.
I come to You.
Please come to me.
Amen.

PRAYER FOR FAITH

Dear God,
May I have faith.
May I not be tempted to forget Your power.
May I not be tempted to forget Your love.
May my mind not stray to the might of the
    destroyer but remember instead the might of
    the Lord.
Tomorrow, You shall show me.
You shall have the last word, the final say.
And so I shall not worry.
You shall redeem me,
I shall resurrect.
You shall bring forth new life from all apparent
    death.

You create from what the darkness has
 destroyed, for Your power is infinite, Your
 forgiveness total, Your mercy complete.
So shall it be that I might fall, but I shall not
 remain down for my Lord is with me.
He shall lift me up.
He shall create a new day.
He shall bring me home.
Praise God.
Amen.

FILLING THE EMPTINESS

"I hate Sundays when I'm not in love," a friend once told me. "They seem so empty. I get depressed."

Most people want the weekend to get here, but some people want the weekend to be over. The workaholic and others addicted to the adrenaline rush of a frantic world cannot bear the burden of Sunday's emptiness. Empty spaces can be unbearable before we discover the power of silence.

This world desperately needs silence. Most people are addicted to stress-producing stimuli. Mentally and emotionally, we need to fast, to clean out the system, to stop overloading it with mean and unnatural mental pollution. We are deeply afraid of the silence, the void, the emptiness. That is because a materialistic prejudice thinks that what cannot be touched does not exist. The void is not material; it is *force.*

The void is where God is. Empty places, empty moments are not really empty; they're pregnant. God is the potential fullness gushing out from every empty space, the ever-present possibility of a magic moment or miraculous thought. Off the blank page jumps a cosmic summons. Out of that silence came the opening chords of Beethoven's Fifth.

A person is like a circle surrounded by the entire world. That's often how we feel—like limited spaces surrounded by infinity. We try to consume the external, to give us a feeling of internal satisfaction. And yet we cannot satisfy that yearning, because nothing outside of us is the stuff for which we hunger. The more we grab, the less centered we are. And so we disintegrate; we do not grow. We take on the characteristics of neurotic, needy people, for that is the road we decide to follow whenever we look to the world for what the world cannot give us.

It is imperative, therefore, that we give time each day, each week, to silence, to the internal search, to honoring God before the world.

We must embrace the void instead of resisting it. That is the way of the mystic. It is the only way we can heal.

⎯⎯

Dear God,

I resist meditation, I resist prayer, I resist my spiritual practice at times, for I am not comfortable with the empty spaces.

I know, dear God, that I am out of balance with my spiritual nature.

I need to be healed.

Please heal me.

Bring me to the silence within myself, and give me comfort there.

Show me the fierce and quiet center of Your love, which is within me.

Thank You very much.

Amen.

GROUP PRAYER
FOR GOD'S PRESENCE

We invite Him in now,
He who is already here,
To burst forth into our awareness and into our
    human experience,
More deeply, more powerfully, more substan-
    tially than ever before.
We no longer look to the wings of a sparrow to
    carry us,
But we look to the wings of the eagle within us.
Dear God, please carry us home.
Amen.

4

Prayers for the Body

We are returning, as a collective awareness, to the understanding that the body is in fact not separate from the mind. As we relinquish our primitive mechanistic perspective and appreciate again the influence of the soul, we embrace a different attitude toward the body. The body is a reflection of thought. God's thought is our salvation in all things. His thought about the body is that it is here for one function: to experience love and to extend love, to help communicate to the children of God that true life is, in fact, beyond the body. The body is a holy lesson in communion and should be seen and treated as a sacred trust. Thoughts of aggression, unforgiveness, conflict and fear, tear down the body because they tear down the soul. Healed thoughts produce healing, in body as well as mind.

GRATITUDE FOR THE BODY

Dear God,
As I rise up, I thank You for the opportunity to
   be on this earth.
I thank You for my mind and body.
I thank You for my life.
Please bless my body and use it for Your pur-
   poses.
May I rise up strong today, and may my body
   and soul radiate Your love.
May all impurities be cast out of my mind, my
   heart, my body.
May every cell of my being be filled with Your
   light.
May my body and mind both be illumined for
   Your sake and for the sake of all the world.
Amen.

PRAYERS FOR HEALING

Dear God,
My body is sick and I am so scared, so weak, so
    sad.
Please heal me, Lord.
Whatever the words I am supposed to say,
    whatever the thoughts that would set me free,
I am willing to have them shine into my mind.
For I wish to be released.
Please give me a miracle.
Please give me hope.
Please give me peace.
Lift me up beyond the regions of my pain and
    despair.
Prepare each cell to be born anew into health
    and happiness, peace and love.
For You are the power, not this sickness.
You are the truth, not this illusion.
You are my salvation, not the doctor.
I am willing to rise, to let go all false thinking,
    to release this false condition.
For this is not freedom, and I wish to be free.
This is not peaceful, and I desire peace.

This is not Your will for me, that I would suffer
    or feel pain.
I accept Your will for me.
I accept Your healing.
I accept Your love.
Please, dear God, help me.
Take me home.
Amen.

                                ~⌒⌒~

Dear God,
Please awaken me from this dream.
I fear and I choose not to,
I suffer and I choose not to.
I claim for myself Your resurrection within me,
    my perfect health, my perfect healing, my
    perfect Self in whom there is no pain or fear.
Every cell of my being is radiant with my love
    for You.
May my earthly self align with this,
May my human heart stop beating so wildly.
May I remember, dear God, that I live in Your
    mind and I belong in Your arms.
For there I am healed, and there I am whole.

You are my divine physician.

You know my terror, although it is not real.

You understand my pain, although it is not
understandable.

You answer with Your spirit.

Dear Lord, please heal me.

I surrender this as I surrender all things

I trust in You in this and all things

I need You, Lord, in this and all things.

Please, dear God.

Amen.

PRAYER FOR
A PARTNER'S HEALING
(*You may wish to place your hands upon
the body of the sick.*)

In the name of God, who is within me, I accept
His power with gratitude.

I open my heart and my hands to receive it.

Beloved brother, may this power reach you.

May you be healed.

Every cell of my being, every thought in my
mind is radiant with Grace.

Through my hands, there now flows to you His
power and His Love.

You are forgiven, for you were not condemned.

You are healed, for you shall now know your
innocence.

You are whole.

You are healed.

God sees you this way.

As I accept Him more deeply into my heart, I
accept for myself His vision of you.

I see only your perfection.

I see only your love.

I see not your past.

I see not your mistakes.

I see not your disease.

I see not your pain.

For they have been cast out through the grace of
God.

Through the mercy of the Lord, through the
wonder of the universe, which loves us all
and gives new life, may you be blessed and be
made new.

You are healed.

You are whole.

And so it is.

Amen.

ADDICTIONS

We are people who have lost our peace. Having lost it, we look for it everywhere. We more than look: In fact, we grab desperately. Until we remember that our own capacity to love is what we truly seek, we are doomed to endless compulsion to look for happiness where there is none and for satisfaction where there is only more longing.

Only a spiritual experience can sober us.

⁓

Dear God,
I cannot stop:
- drinking
- using
- eating
- (*say your own*)

I have tried.
I have tried so hard.
And still, Lord, I go back and do it, though I
    hate myself for doing it.
I cannot stop.
I cannot stop.

You, dear Lord, are my refuge and security and
    strength when I cannot go on.

Please lift me up and share Your strength with me.

Please lift from me this burden, the burden of
    this addiction, the pain of this self-hatred,
    the power of this demon within me.

I do not have the power on my own to fight this
    beast.

But You, dear Lord, You do.

You do.

I praise Your strength and power and love.

Please give it to me.

Please take away my desire to:

· drink

· use

· eat immoderately

· (*say your own*)

Please take it away.

Please take it away.

I surrender all.

I lay myself in Your arms.

Please give me a miracle.

Thank you.

Thank you.

Thank you.

Amen.

AGE

(See also *Ceremony of the Elder:
A Rite of Midlife*)

One of the most unfortunate weaknesses in the life cycle of our generation is our failure to honor age. As we mature past the obsessions of our earlier years and grapple with the meaning of our own midlife, we face the karmic payback to our past overemphasis on the value of youth. We must rediscover and recast the meaning and importance of the mature, the elder, the wise one. The generation that led the revolution of the sixties is no longer young; we have at last grown up. We must lead the new revolution as well, not in beautiful, rebellious outrage but in beautiful, moral outrage.

Our fear of age will be cast out as we once more begin to respect it.

❧

Dear God,
I am getting older.
It fills me with fear,
For I live in a world with no respect for aging.

Show me how to see it differently,
That I might feel its strength and beauty and
    power within me:
Its power for good, its power for wisdom, its
    power for knowledge, its power for leadership.
May I become wise.
I receive into my heart the sacred elders.
May their greater experience and greater aware-
    ness make them my teachers and my guides.
I realize it is a sacred privilege to care for them,
As they in their time have cared for me.
Please transform my experience of age.
Show me its possibilities for greatness.
Release me from my fear.
Amen.

DEATH

Opening up to the pain of death, our own or
that of someone we love, is one of the most mys-
terious blessings of life. Nothing focuses us
more clearly on what matters, helps us drop our
defenses more quickly or gives us more compassion for human suffering.

I used to think that the Angel of Death would be a terrible thing. I realize now that the Angel of Death would have to be God's most tender and understanding angel, to be sent to us at such a significant, frightening juncture. There are many among us now who have seen the Angel of Death or have had to start thinking about it before our time. Death has become one of our greatest teachers in the transition to a spiritually awakened world.

"Death shall be the last enemy," said Jesus. What He meant was that we would no longer perceive death as an enemy. We would recognize that death is not death but a recycling of energy, a remodulation of the cells according to higher assignments in a soul's progression. The spirit does not die, but rather enters new channels of life.

The power of God is greater than death. Our relationships are not severed at death, but refocused beyond physical connection. As our vision of life changes, so will the physical world. As we lift our eyes above the illusion of death, we will begin to see the eternity of life.

Jesus did not die when He died, and neither do we.

PRAYER FOR A PEACEFUL DEATH

Dear God,
I think that I am going to die.
I think I'm going to leave this world.
Give me strength, Lord, that I might not fear.
I know, dear God, that when I leave I do not
    die, that when I die I shall continue to live
    in Your arms, in Your mind, in Your spirit
    forever.
And yet, dear Lord, my heart beats wildly.
I am so scared.
My heart breaks to be leaving those I love: my
    friends, my mate, my children, my loves.
And yet I know I shall not be leaving.
Heal my heart that I might know this.
Heal theirs also that they might know that we
    are bound together forever, through your
    power, which is greater than the power of
    death.
For the arms of God are the arms of life.
Dear God, I surrender my body to You.
If it serves Your purposes, then may I live,
And if the arc of destiny now calls me home,
    then let me die in peace, dear God.

Send the Angel of Death to me when it is my
  time.
Let me feel the Angel's tenderness as I exit this
  world and enter the next.
Let me go from dark to light.
Let me feel the love of God.
Please comfort me and those I love.
Now while I wait, now while I face my fears and
  my pain,
Let me see the truth and know Your peace.
May my family and friends now feel the same.
For we shall not be torn asunder.
Our love is larger than death.
Our bond is eternal.
Your life is with us always.
So I believe, so shall I feel, now and forever.
Hallelujah, Lord.
For Yours is the power and the glory and love.
You are with me as I am with You
Thank you, God, for what has been.
Thank you, God, for what shall be.
Forgive me my darkness.
Reveal to me Your light.
Bless my family.
Take care of them, my darling ones.

Take me home.

I willingly surrender.

I shall not fear, for You are with me.

Thank you, Lord.

Thank you, Lord.

Thank you, Lord.

Amen.

PRAYER FOR THE DEAD
(See also *Memorial Service*)

Dear God,

Please take the soul and spirit of this dear
departed one into the sweetest corner of
Your mind, the most tender place in Your
heart, that she, and I, might be comforted.

For now she has gone, and I pray, dear God, for
the strength to remember she has not gone
far.

For she is with You and shall remain so forever.

She remains within me, for we are all in You
together.

The cord that binds us one to the other cannot
be cut, surely not by death.

For You, dear God, have brought us together,
    and we remain in eternal connection.
There is no power greater than You.
Death is not Your master, nor mine.
These things I believe and ask my heart to
    register.
I surrender to You my grief.
I surrender to You my pain.
Please take care of Your servant, my dear one
    who has passed.
And please, dear Lord, take care of me.
Amen.

5

Prayers for Relationships

Relationships are our primary teacher. They are the context in which we either grow into God consciousness, or deny ourselves and others the opportunity to do so.

There are simple keys to happy relationships, which is not to say that these keys are always easy to use. One key to abundance in every area of life is this: We experience God's peace and harmony to the extent to which we love, forgive, and focus on the good in others and in ourselves.

We ask God to help us do that, so that relationships that are new will be good, ones that are good will keep getting better, and ones that are broken will be repaired. God's law is that we love one another. Obeying that law is the key to a happy life.

None of this means that we then lack the capacity to set boundaries, say a healthy "no," or stand up for ourselves when we need to. Quite the opposite: Since love aligns us with the thoughts of God, it aligns us with our personal power. Where there is total love, there is no guilt. Where there is no guilt, there is no obstruction to true and honest communication.

What truly serves one person's good serves the good of all. We don't have to decide whether to love others at the expense of ourselves or ourselves at the expense of others, because ultimately we are all one. There are no separate needs, for there are no separate beings except in illusion. Understanding that paradox gives us a healthy sense of our own individuality, for it gives us a sense of ourselves based on love and not defensiveness. A healthy self-love is not narcissistic but self-extending. We are all waves in the same ocean and sunbeams of the same sun. Only in illusion are we separate, and we pray to transcend illusion. We pray to be able to perceive our oneness with others, with God, and within ourselves.

The idea that someone is supporting us when they foster our belief in another person's guilt is false. All minds are joined. That is the meaning of the Sonship. Whatever thoughts we hold toward others we are holding about ourselves as well. It is only in relinquishing our focus on another person's guilt that we can know the joy of our own innocence.

From that place, we can say a very powerful "no" when necessary. We can tell them not to call anymore, we can take back the house keys, we can even call a lawyer if that's what it takes. Love is not weakness, but wisdom. God's answer is always loving, but the loving answer is not always "yes."

Relationships are the central issue in a peaceful, powerful life. The following prayers are guidelines for helping you get on the ladder to heaven, helping you stay there, and helping you climb.

Dear God,
Show me the light at the center of my brothers.
Show me the light at the center of myself.
Show me the light at the center of the world.
Where I see guilt, show me innocence.
Where I focus on mistakes, show me how to
    focus on efforts at good.
Help me have faith in the goodness of others.
Help me have faith in Your spirit within me.
Thus may darkness be cast out.
May I cleave to the light that is my heart.
This is my prayer.
May I see the light in everyone.
Amen.

LOVED ONES

Praying for someone is a gracious act. It gives blessing to the one who prays, as well to the person who is prayed for.

Every day, during times of prayer, let us think of the people in our lives we love most. Let us remember our children, our parents, our siblings. Let us consciously thank God that they exist, and ask for holiness in our relationships with them.

Imagine life to be like a camera: The amount of light in the picture is determined by the size of the aperture at the time the picture is taken. For most of us most of the time, our experience of life and its potential for joy is severely limited by the constriction of our own hearts. It's as though an aperture is shut, at least partially, that could be completely open. The joy we seek lies less in something new happening and more in our opening our hearts more fully to the love in our lives already. Only love can make us happy, and only we ourselves can determine its presence or absence inside our hearts. To acknowledge love is to increase its capacity to heal us; to ignore love is to let it slip away.

Look around you while you are in public somewhere or gathered with loved ones. Look into the faces of the people you see, and silently say: "The light of God in me salutes the light of God in you." Do it for five minutes, minimum. I defy you to do this each day for at least five minutes and *not* be happy.

Do this in traffic when you are frustrated, while in line at the Department of Motor Vehicles, while sitting in a restaurant. We find our happiness to the extent to which we use our minds to bless the world, for using our minds this way is the reason we were born.

As much as we would all love to be thoroughly loving all the time, we would be less than honest if we claimed we are. In fact, we are all thrown curve balls in the form of people and situations we are tempted to judge. How otherwise would we grow but by growing through such challenges to our capacity to love?

Our prayer work demands that we be rigorously honest with ourselves and God. We must be willing, with His help, to pluck from our minds every nonloving, critical, judgmental thought. Have a go.

Let's begin with the world in general. Let's look in our hearts for any prejudice or intolerance. Where we find ourselves with a bigoted thought toward someone else's religion, nationality, color, or political orientation, let us ask God to remove those thoughts, to rid our minds of any hatred or judgment.

"No," you might say, "I am not a bigot," and perhaps you are not. But who among us can honestly say, "I do not judge"? Let us take this moment, now, to consider the places where we hold the sword of judgment over someone, and in this moment, let us pray to be healed.

It is important, in saying such a prayer, that we get specific in admitting our own darkness. Below are a list of possible targets for judgments or prejudices that we still might hold:

Blacks	Asians
Whites	Buddhists
American Indians	Muslims
WASPs	Hindus
Jews	Men
New Agers	Women
Catholics	Democrats
Protestants	Republicans
Born-again	Liberals
Christians	Conservatives
Non-born-again	Capitalists
Christians	Socialists
Religious people	Atheists
Old people	Agnostics
Hispanics	Religious people
Europeans	The rich
Americans	The poor

Communists	Heterosexuals
Northerners	Homosexuals
Southerners	

Need I say more? Let us continue to search our own minds for the hidden places where we still deny love. Perhaps we learned loveless attitudes from our parents, or from experiences in the past. Wherever we picked up judgmental attitudes, they do not serve us now. They do not serve God or the creation of a new world, and serving God is our only goal. To serve God is to think with love. In prayerful request, let us give up all thoughts that are not of love.

Every morning, every evening, let us search our minds for the judgments we still hold, for the unforgivenesses, the places where we do not love. The ego is sly and insidious. It takes discipline and vigilance to do the mental work necessary to purify our hearts. Honesty with ourselves and God, and the willingness to be healed by Him, form the crux of the pilgrim's journey.

Dear God,

I surrender to You my thoughts of judgment.

Please heal me of my temptation to blame Your
children whom You adore.

Teach me to love as You do.

Teach me to see the reality behind the superficial masks, the truth in the hearts of all Your
children.

May I see the innocence in all humanity, that I
may see the world of Your creation, the
world anew, the world that shall be.

I relinquish my miscreations.

I surrender my belief in guilt.

Bring me home to the truth at last.

May all God's children be innocent in my eyes,
for they are all my brothers.

May I see this that the world might heal.

Dear God,

Give me new eyes, Your eyes.

Amen.

FORGIVENESS

The vision of God's spirit is the vision of innocence. It is not our job to forgive whom God has not condemned, but rather to remember that God condemns no one.

God heals through forgiveness and asks that we do likewise. Attack is an easier response than forgiveness, and that is why we are so tempted to give into it. Throughout our lives, we have seen more anger than examples of true forgiveness. Forgiveness does not mean we suppress our anger; forgiveness means that we have asked for a miracle: the ability to see through the mistakes that someone has made to the truth that lies in all of our hearts. None of this "I'm too spiritual to be angry," for who among us is? Rather, we pray, "I am angry, dear God. But I am willing not to be. I am willing to see this situation another way."

Forgiveness is not always easy. At times, it feels more painful than the wound we suffered, to forgive the one who inflicted it.

And yet, there is no peace without forgiveness. Attack thoughts toward others are attacks on

ourselves. The first step in forgiveness is the willingness to forgive. If you can state, despite your
resistance, your willingness to see the spiritual
innocence, the light in the soul of one who has
harmed you, you have begun the journey to a
deep and unshakable peace.

⟨෨⟩

Dear God,
There is someone whom I very much dislike.
It is: (*say your own*).
My anger or unforgiveness is because: (*say your
own*).
I know that my ability to forgive this person is
where my freedom lies, for my hatred and
judgment are attacks upon myself.
This hatred keeps me tied, dear Lord, to the
guilt within my mind, and I am willing to be
free.
Dear God, please help me.
I surrender to You my thoughts of this person's
guilt.
I allow myself to fully feel my pain, my sense of
violation,

My fear that this person will hurt me again.

I take these feelings and place them in Your
hands.

May Your love be like a bonfire in which my
feelings can transform.

I know my attack thoughts are hurting me,

And yet I feel I cannot let them go.

And so I say to You, dear Lord, I am willing to
see this person's innocence.

I am willing to see the pain in him that would
make him do these things.

I am willing to have my perceptions healed that
I might rise above, that I might hurt no
longer, that I might be released from this
wheel of suffering.

For I know if I could drop this, I would be set
free.

I cannot do this for myself, Dear Lord.

In spite of my pain, in spite of my resistance,

I pray for this person.

I ask that this person be healed and given new
life,

As I ask for surcease from my own pain.

For truly we are reborn or we die together.

I know this.

I am willing to have a miracle.

I am willing to forgive.

I need Your strength to do so.

Thank You, Lord, for making me bigger, for
bringing me closer to the divine power in my
own heart.

I surrender this person to You.

I surrender my pain to You.

Heal him.

Heal me.

Thank You.

Amen.

ANGER

What is not love is fear. Anger is one of fear's
most potent faces. And it does exactly what fear
wants it to do: It keeps us from receiving love at
exactly the moment when we need it most.

Our greatest need, when fearful, is to be able
to express how scared we are. Instead, of course,
we are often tempted to express anger, meekly
hoping that somehow, someone will read our
minds and say "I know you're only angry because

you feel so scared. Come here and I'll love you."
There are those rare moments when the other
person is evolved enough to do that; in the vast
majority of cases, however, our anger will send
others further and further away from us, increasing our pain and increasing our terror.

What we give to others stays with us. That is
true of both love and fear. Anger, then, is not to
be denied but surrendered to God. Our prayer is
to be shown an alternative way of conflict resolution. We want both to be in touch with our
anger and to release our anger. What we do not
want is to project our anger onto someone else in
the false belief that we will then feel better. Such
behavior offers only temporary relief. Before
we express our anger to others, the attitude of
empowerment is to express our anger as well as
our pain to God. He can handle it. The line
"Vengeance is mine, sayeth the Lord" actually
means just that.

When the anger mounts, call on God. Tell
Him first.

Dear God,

Take from me my rage.

I feel such anger from my pain, my frustration, and my disappointment.

I throw my anger in so many inappropriate places.

I do not contain it or use it creatively.

Dear God,

Please grant me serenity and peace that I might know my power within my peace.

Transmute my rage, transform my anger that I might not direct it against others or myself,

That it might be undone,

Unraveled through the grace of God.

Where I am focusing on someone's guilt, please show me his innocence, for I know that my attack on him is my own damnation.

I am willing to see everyone's innocence.

Please show it to me.

Thank you.

Bless us all.

Amen.

Dear God,

I have been betrayed.

Take away from me this pain.

Let me not be tempted to wrong those who have
wronged me, or to hate those who hate me.

But rather, dear God, please use Your power on
my behalf,

That through Your love I might invoke the light,

That through Your forgiveness I might speed
resurrection,

That through Your grace the spirit of the Lord
might enter and make all things right.

Let me not be tempted by darkness, even
though it is all around me.

Let me continue to see the good in others,

Even when they have turned the arrows of their
fear at me.

Be my shield, dear Lord.

And please be my protector.

Awaken in others the truth in their hearts.

And awaken the same in me.

I have faith in You, dear God, to right all
wrongs, to make all things clear, to bring
light out of apparent darkness.

I hold to You.
I bless those who have not blessed me.
I forgive them and I forgive myself.
Or so do I wish to do.
I ask for Your help.
I pray for comfort.
Thank You very much.
Amen.

FRIENDSHIP

True friendship reveals itself in time—not only in the sense of time spent together getting to know one another, but also in the sense that it is through the ravages as well as the easier times in life that we come to see, as they say, "who our friends are."

Loyalty to friends is easy when nothing rotten is in the air. But when rumors are flying, or innuendos, or betrayals—that is when the quality of true friendship becomes the stuff of heroic response. To give a friend the benefit of the doubt, to listen with depth and compassion and nonjudgment to his story, to remain an approving friend even when you do not agree with a particular position, to be truly loyal in an age where loyalty is so easily relinquished—these are opportunities to use friendship as a means of righteous participation in life.

We live at a time when people collect friends like we collect clothes—different types for different moods, seasonal, disposable. Friends should be like classics, having nothing to do with this season's trends or appetites or designs. They should be a mainstay of life, not only for what we get from them personally, but also for the opportunities they provide us to practice the art of a more noble existence.

True friends are not easily forsworn. In today's society, we often put our selfish interests first, before integrity or loyalty or commitment to higher principles. This is ultimately not a winning attitude, for what emanates from us will be back at our door in time. Too often we didn't learn in childhood that honor is important, that we must do what is right for the sake of doing what is right. Too often our childhood experiences left us completely devoid of role models who showed us what it meant to care actively and nonexploitatively for the welfare of other people.

Commitment to a noble relationship is a hard road at times. It means saying "I would rather not get the job if it means that I have to conspire in wronging a friend" or "I will stand up publicly in defense of my friend, even if there is a groundswell of misunderstanding surrounding him" or "I would rather not have that money, if to receive it would mean that my friend gets hurt" or "I will not get romantically involved with that person, if it means that the heart of my friend would be wounded."

We are overcasual about friendship because we are overcasual about everything. Friends are our extended family. Their good is inextricably bound up with ours. Our concern for their good is our concern for ourselves. This does not mean that we are here to enable, but it does mean that we are here to care and to care actively. Too many times, we set boundaries that are boundaries against our own willingness to love. What is the purpose of being a friend if we don't take seriously the responsibility of supporting someone?

Support system means just that: that members of the system support one another. Of course we

value independence, and friendship is not meant
to undermine that value in ourselves or others.
But still, in the strongest of personalities, in the
most blessed of lives, there are times when a person emotionally falls down. Where are we then, if
not for our friends? Who else can we depend on,
to lend the resources of kindness and strength to
help us get back up? Friendship should not be
taken lightly. It is as sacred a commitment as any
other; our friends are sent by God, for us to help
them and for them to help us.

We live in meanspirited times. People instinc-
tively attack. There's often more criticism leveled
against success than failure, more suspicion of
excellence than of mediocrity. We do not live in a
friendly society. A friend assumes our innocence.
A friend applauds our desire to play big in life. A
friend supports our efforts to live according to
spiritual purpose. A friend is always ready to help
us forgive. A friend forgives us when we need forgiveness.

A friend will see us at our worst, as well as at
our best, but his love will not waver when we have
failed to show our most positive features. A
friend will not close his heart when we have made

a mistake. A friend will not condemn us but will compassionately support our return to a state of grace. Friends will try to refrain from criticism, because it hurts the friendship and it hurts the soul.

The conscious prayer is not "Dear God, send me more friends" but rather "Dear God, make me a good friend." Do I appreciate my friends or do I take them for granted? Do I let them know how grateful I am? Do I actively, verbally support them in their endeavors? Do I give to my friends, or do I do more taking?

Let us pray.

❧

Dear God,
With this prayer, I call to mind my friends.
I ask for Your blessing on them.
May angels fill their nights and bless their days.
May they find joy and peace and harmony.
May I be a source of happiness in their lives.
May our bond be strong and based on truth.
May they always know that in me, they have
    support.

May I live a life that lives up to this prayer.
Thank You, God.
Amen.

PRAYER BETWEEN FRIENDS

Dear God,
We surrender this relationship to You.
May it serve Your purposes and be blessed by
    You always.
Fill our minds with Your thoughts.
May we always be led to the highest vision of
    each other.
Remove any obstruction to our highest love.
Thank You very much.
Amen.

WHEN CONFLICT HAPPENS

If your relationship is experiencing difficulty, the
other person may be willing to join with you in
prayer. Even if he or she is not, however, prayer is
still the answer.

If one person invites God's spirit into a situation, then His spirit enters.

⟿⟿

Dear God,
Please reveal our love to us, for now it is
    obscured.
Bring us peace and healing, for we are lost in the
    darkness of conflict and separation.
We surrender to You our attacks and defenses.
We relinquish all perceptions that we bring
    from the past.
We surrender to You our positions and agendas.
Please help us see love.
Please bring us back to the path of peace.
Cleanse our minds of all but helpful thoughts.
May our relationship be reborn through Your
    spirit and grace.
We apologize for: (*say your own*).
We forgive the following: (*say your own*).
Please clear our path that we might see again,
    the light that is our love for each other.
Thank You very much.
Amen.

FALLING IN LOVE

Falling in love has been getting a bad rap recently. Supposedly more sophisticated types suggest that falling in love is an illusion, a state of non-reality because it is based on failure to see the love object as a "real" human being. According to this view, "real" love sets in only at the end of infatuation. A beautiful smile or dreams of greatness, for instance, are not considered as *real* as one's tendency to squeeze the toothpaste from the top of the tube.

From an illumined perspective, falling in love is not neurotic but rather one of the few genuinely nonneurotic things we do on this earth. Falling in love is an effort to retrieve Paradise, that dimension of bliss where no one is blamed for anything and everyone is fully appreciated for who they are. When we fall in love, we drop for however brief a time our tendency to judge. We suspend our disbelief and eschew our faithlessness in another human being.

What usually happens after that is not that we finally wake up to reality. What tends to happen after that is that we *fall asleep* to reality. We cannot wake up to our brother's imperfections, because the perception of imperfection is itself a non-awakened state. Our spiritual perfection is not altered by our imperfect personalities. Seeing perfection is seeing the light. Falling in love is not an illusion, as much as falling *out* of love is a fall from grace.

What we see when we fall in love is not illusion but truth. We want to fall in love because we want so much to return to God. Of course we want to escape this darkened world. We want desperately to go home to a place where all of us can see how beautiful we all are.

Some people say that falling in love is a state of denial. It is, actually. In love, we are in a *positive* denial—a denial of darkness. What then occurs is that we start to believe the serpent's lies—we begin to see good and evil: "I like him, but he doesn't make enough money" or "I like her, but she's too high maintenance." Spirit has celebrated how wonderful they are; now the negative mind gets to celebrate how *guilty* they are. Guilt is the ego's orgasm.

Most people do not have the personality structure to hold on to the strength it takes to love without judgment. And so love's magic dies, casting Adam and Eve out of Paradise.

As our minds are illumined, we become better at romance because we become better at being human. We become better at forgiveness and support and love. The enlightened world will not be one in which no one ever falls in love. The enlightened world will be one in which everyone is in love with everyone all the time. There will be no judgment, therefore no blocks to the awareness of love. We will see each other as God created us: as the perfect, loving and lovable people we really are at our core. The purpose of romantic love is to jump start our enlightenment.

∽✦∾

Dear God,
I am ready to see perfection in another human
  being.
I am ready to surrender all my thoughts of how
  my partner isn't good enough.
I am ready to see the beauty in the inner core of
  all mankind.

If there is one person, either in my life or on
their way, who would benefit from my vision
of her loveliness, let her make her way into
my arms.
May my perception of her beauty wash away
her self-hatred.
May my forgiveness of her errors release her
from her guilt.
May I learn to support, to listen, to understand.
May I learn to serve her in her quest for higher
ground.
May I learn to give joy, to nurture and to share.
And most of all, may I never forget to pray for
my love and help her pray.
Amen.

ROMANCE

There is a difference between romance and love.
Often the true path of love begins only when
romance has begun to taper off, for love is the
capacity to see light when darkness has begun to
eclipse it. Love is easy when romance still lights
everything in shades of pink, when the experi-

ence of a relationship is like the canvas of a sweet Impressionistic painting. Once the reality of our woundings reveals the darkness still lurking in all of us, romance might die, while true love does not.

Many people are proficient at romance who are not proficient at love. They see the humanness of their partner and say, Nah, I want romance again. Then they start over elsewhere, beginning again the path that will always end up in the exact same place.

The choice to follow love through to its completion is the choice to seek completion within ourselves. The point at which we shut down on others is the point at which we shut down on life. We heal as we heal others, and we heal others by extending our perceptions past their weaknesses. Until we have seen someone's darkness, we don't really know who that person is. Until we have forgiven someone's darkness, we don't really know what love is. Forgiving others is the only way to forgive ourselves, and forgiveness is our greatest need. Running away from someone else's darkness is a way of running away from our own, in the false belief that in running we can escape.

But we cannot escape. Our self-loathing will always meet us down the road, no matter how fast we run and what fancy footwork we're doing. Failure to see our judgment of others as an extension of our judgment of ourselves denies healing to both people—until the next time the lesson comes around, which it will.

Without forgiveness, love has no meaning. It has no fullness or maturity. Only when two people have shown each other the worst side of our natures are we truly ready for the task of love. Then we're ready to begin. How tragic it is that so often we stop everything just as we reach the starting line.

That is why we must always pray to see the truth about a relationship: not just our truth but God's truth. "May God's will be done, not my own" is the prayer for ultimate fulfillment because it seeks an emotionally higher ground than the fulfillment of our immature desires. We must move past the narcissistic preoccupation with getting the love we think "works" for us. The point of love is to make us grow, not to make us immediately happy.

Many of us have forsworn the chance for the deepest love in reaching out for the easier one.

PRAYER TO ATTRACT
GREAT LOVE

Dear God,

I feel an empty space within me, a place where I
would so love to love.

I know that if my beloved came here, I would
adore and cherish, honor and serve him.

Please give me the opportunity to expand my
heart into the life of another in the holiest
way, the most beautiful way, the most intimate way, if that serves Your purpose.

For I would learn the secrets of love and use
what I learn to grace the life of another.

What a marvelous possibility, Lord, that such a
treasure would be placed in my hands.

Please do this.

I will try my best.

Amen.

INTIMACY

The purpose of intimate partnership is for us to
midwife the perfection in each other. The point

of love is to reveal to us the light inside. This is the lesson we are meant to learn and that in one way or another we will learn.

If we are unconscious about these issues, if we fail to live up to the sacred challenges of loving another person, then we will experience disastrous relationships, and the disasters will motivate us to grow. If we are conscious and careful, then we will experience the processes of growth through the joys of love instead of pain. It is said in the Kaballah, the Jewish system of mystical wisdom, that leaning over every blade of grass there is an angel saying, "Grow, grow, grow." There is that same angel over every relationship, shoving us into the next stage of our development whether we are cracked open by light or cracked open by despair. We have a choice whether or not to love, but we have no choice whether or not to grow.

Our intimate love is our partner on a holy adventure. With this person, we are given the chance to move into the center of things. In the spiritual space of intimate connection, we have the power to heal and be healed.

In order to be healed, we must reveal our wounds. And so it is that the person with whom we share the deepest love is often the one with whom we share the deepest pain. For when we hold a person deeply in our hearts, we hold their darkness as well as their light. We must accept both faces. The ability to accept our partner's darkness and our willingness to reveal our own make us vulnerable to wounding. But these are sacred wounds; they are prelude to sacred healing.

Intimacy doesn't mean that both people are perfect. It doesn't even mean that one person is perfect. It means that two people understand that we are all wounded and we are all here to be healed. The key to empowerment in any area is understanding its purpose, and the purpose of intimacy is healing.

Honoring our connection to another person is a way of honoring God. A relationship is more of an assignment than a choice. A powerful connection between two people is a potent psychic factor that exists regardless of either person's opinion about the relationship. We can walk away from the assignment, but we cannot walk away from the lessons it presents. Sweeping challenges under the rug doesn't get rid of problems; because the universe is hologramatic, failure to complete in one area will always be reflected elsewhere. We stay with a relationship until a lesson is learned or we simply learn it another way. If honest communication between two people isn't extended to the point of resolution and peace, the energy will attach itself to the psyche of both people and appear again as wounding in another relationship.

Intimacy is depth of learning. The Bible doesn't say that Adam and Eve were together for a long time, but it does say that they were naked and unembarrassed. Intimacy means that we're naked and free. Sometimes in that nakedness, what we reveal is how far apart we are. If we're afraid to reveal that, the distance remains. Intimacy means we're safe enough to reveal the truth in all its creative chaos; that is how the wounds of mankind are exorcised. If a space is created in which two people are totally free to reveal their walls, those walls, in time, come down.

Commitment is not just to the other person, but to the experience of truth. Our goal is not perfect form, but perfect content. We mustn't try to get a relationship to fit into our ego's plans, but rather to learn how the relationship fits into

God's plans. Only honest communication can guide us in that pursuit. I once said to a couple, "I have no idea if you are supposed to be together. But neither do you know. There's not enough honesty between you at this point for either one of you to be trusting your opinion either way." On any given day that the truth is not communicated between a couple, the couple builds up negative mass that will explode in their faces in time.

Many times we don't share the truth because we're afraid it would upset the other person to hear how we feel: "I'm feeling claustrophic," "I feel ignored," etc. Negative emotions, however, have a place in intimacy. They need to be revealed in order to be detoxed. Having negative emotions doesn't make us bad. Thinking that they do is what keeps so many people from exposing their emotions. It is when our feelings—all our feelings—are revealed appropriately and then forgiven that we have a chance to heal. Feelings need to be accepted as they are, before they can transform. In the presence of light—and nonjudgmental listening *is* light—all truth moves on to a higher level.

We needn't ever worry that if we really get to the truth in a situation, the truth might be dark. The opposite is true. The *ultimate* truth is always light, because all things end up in God. It is repressed truth that is dark. When negativity is kept inside, it smolders and festers and ultimately finds its way into dysfunctional and destructive expression. As soon as you start trying to hide your darkness, you are bound to hide your light.

This is the spiritual meaning of intimacy: growth inward, past our masks and fears and recklessness, to the sacred place where we are naked before God and each other. On our journey home, we go past many false faces on ourselves and our beloved. Intimacy is where we are willing to move so deeply into love that the demons do not deter us from our conviction to make it through to the light. How tragic it is, that we often turn our faces from each other when the work of healing has only just begun. We must not confuse the face of the devil with too much water under the bridge. For it is when the darkness has started its terrible drumrolls that the wise person knows to attend and take care.

The light is never very far behind, if only we will be willing now to stay on the path of the open heart. The key to intimacy is the commitment to honesty and to the radical forgiveness necessary in order for honesty to be safe. Forgiveness and acceptance are the powers that heal us. Intimacy means we will not forgo the possibility of further connection. We commit not only to tell the truth, but to be willing to listen without judgment and to the best of our ability without hysteria. We allow each moment to organically move into the next, without interference from our fearful posturing.

We must have more faith in the power of love to eternally renew itself than in the power of fear to tear us asunder. The spirit does not turn away from human frailty or conflict, but sees them merely as wounds to heal.

Intimacy challenges us to seek a higher level of participation than the limited thought forms of romantic delusion or false morality. It seeks authentic engagement before superficial agreements. It means that we will always try to show up for love. It's an adult activity and at times a very difficult pursuit. It takes effort and perseverance and a tolerance for emotional pain, for it is a cutting through of the defenses we have built up over a lifetime. It is a most courageous endeavor, which demands great respect for ourselves and others. The art of intimacy is literally the art of the angels, for it is the art of learning to fly beyond the darkness of the world.

When done poorly, intimacy can lead to great pain. When done well, it strikes the devil in the center of the forehead.

PRAYERS FOR COUPLES

Dear God,
Please make of our relationship a great and holy
    adventure.
May our joining be a sacred space.
May the two of us find rest here, a haven for
    our souls.
Remove from us any temptation to judge one
    another or to direct one another.
We surrender to You our conflicts and our
    burdens.
We know You are our Answer and our rock.
Help us to not forget.

Bring us together in heart and mind as well as
   body.
Remove from us the temptation to criticize or
   be cruel.
May we not be tempted by fantasies and
   projections,
But guide us in the ways of holiness.
Save us from darkness.
May this relationship be a burst of light.
May it be a fount of love and wisdom for us,
   for our family, for our community, for our
   world.
May this bond be a channel for Your love and
   healing, a vehicle of Your grace and power.
As lessons come and challenges grow, let us not
   be tempted to forsake each other.
Let us always remember that in each other we
   have the most beautiful woman, the most
   beautiful man,
The strongest one,
The sacred one in whose arms we are repaired.
May we remain young in this relationship.
May we grow wise in this relationship.
Bring us what You desire for us,
And show us how You would have us be.
Thank You, dear God,

You who are the cement between us.
Thank You for this love.
Amen.

సౌం

Dear God,
Please bring us big life and big love, deep life
 and deep love.
We wish to show up now with pure and noble
 hearts that we might midwife the perfection
 in each other.
May we see each other's greatness and invoke
 each other's light.
We surrender all the ways, both those we are
 aware of and those that remain unconscious,
 in which we block our love for each other.
We surrender our defenses.
We are ready to bring forth the holiest vibrations of love and healing between us.
Where we are afraid to love, where we have built
 walls in front of our hearts, may we be
 healed and set free.
Where we are needy or do not know how to
 behave or tend to control or to judge or to

fix or be dishonest, please, dear God, show us
another way.
We surrender ourselves to love.
We surrender our love to You.
May it serve Your purposes.
May it receive Your blessing and carry Your
power.
May we never forsake each other.
Thank You very much.
Amen.

FEAR OF INTIMACY

Fear of intimacy is a fear of death. In a world
where we have been taught to believe that the
bolstering of our individual power is the greatest
good, it is difficult to feel that a melting of the
walls surrounding us is something to be desired.
In some ways, we are right: Intimacy *does* melt the
walls, it *does* mean the surrender of our heretofore
completely independent mode of operation, and
it *does* decrease the freedom we have to stand
forth in the world as a lone and individual force.
What it does not do, however, is decrease our per-

sonal power. Surrender to love increases personal power for it expands who we are. That is why Jesus said that those who lose their lives shall find their lives. Until we understand this, we are afraid to surrender to love, for we are afraid to die to who we were. We may loathe who we are, yet we still resist the chance to become someone new. It is only when we are ready to embrace the possibility that we might be tomorrow who we were not today that true intimacy becomes attractive. If all you want to do is remain who and what you are now, then by all means don't fall in love.

This is particularly hard to do if a parent smothered us, if their love constricted our freedom or in any other way denied us our own individual life force. There are healthy boundaries and unhealthy ones. Our healthy boundaries must be strong before we are safe to melt. Once our boundaries are strong, however, the refusal to melt is a spiritual weakness. Once you're a solid and strong individual, the next highest step is to surrender it all. What is truly ours can't be taken away. Surrender to love doesn't weaken us but strengthens us. Intimacy doesn't build a bridge to another person, but rather eradicates the illusion that there ever was a gap.

There is nothing wrong with admitting to ourselves and others our reticence to surrender. It is important that we recognize our fear in order to be healed of it. What we want to avoid is signaling that we are ready to surrender when in fact we are not. We must be very strong before we are capable of renouncing that strength in favor of a higher power. The individual is power-ful, but the extension of our love into the life of another is a higher power. Intimacy is a higher power, for it is the joining of two souls, and there God is. That is why intimacy is sacred and why it is such an important and significant task. God heals the world two by two.

Intimacy without surrender is not intimacy, for what we surrender is the armor that keeps us separate. Often we feel we are ready for intimacy when in fact we are not. The ego can be very clever in hiding from our own eyes—much less someone else's—the many and varied games we play in our efforts to dodge love. To the ego, true love of another is death, for the ego is our belief in separation. When the ego has been our partner for so long, it's somewhat difficult to give it up. We feel foolish when we are out from under its cover. What we ultimately learn, of course, is that we are foolish when we are not.

In surrendering we do not lose but only gain. Intimacy means giving up and giving in in order to receive everything. We do not surrender to another person so much as to love itself. Intimacy is a very high-level activity. The immature can grow strong, the immature can love, but only the mature can surrender.

⁓

Dear God,
Please show me how to love.
Teach me how to extend my light into the life of
    another.
Remove the barriers to my soul, the walls which
    stand in front of my heart,
My commitment to aloneness,
My resistances to joining.
I do not seek love, dear God, for I know it is all
    around me.

I seek instead the healing of my resistances to it,
    the strengthening of my spirit;
That I might learn to love, to love well, to love
    fully, to love deeply.
When my true love calls, dear Lord,
Please keep my ears open.
Let me not shut down.
Let me not forsake him.
Let me always remember that his call to love
    him is my call to love You.
Thank You very much.
Amen.

RESISTING LOVE

We all feel at times as though we are deficient in
ways that other people are not. We must keep in
mind that where the road is crooked God makes
it straight, and where our hearts are wounded
God makes us whole. As we open our hearts in
purity and simplicity, admitting to God that we
are completely powerless in the area of our problem, His illumination redeems us.

Who among us is the master at love that we would want to be? Most of us, quite simply, were never taught the skills. We're just beginning to learn how to love and love well.

❧

Dear God,

I feel such a failure at reaching out to love.

Time and time again I have tried to open my
    heart and combine it with another.

And every time, it seems, I come upon the
    frailty and the scars within me.

I need Your power to free me and release me.

My commitment to separation, to being alone,
    to conflict overpower my best intentions.

I try to build the most beautiful connection,
    and so many times I fail.

Dear God,

I surrender to You every idea and every thought
    I hold about relationships.

Transform my thoughts, rearrange my energies.

Make me into a person who knows how to love,
    to give it and to receive it, to honor it and be
    in it.

Erase my past failures.
Make me new.
I need a miracle.
Please.
Amen.

THE MYSTICAL RECONNECTION

Mystical power neither originates from nor acts upon the material realm. It is the sustaining energy of the world beyond—beyond body, argument, reasons or personality. Mystical power in relationships comes not from improving our "people skills" but from developing our "soul skills." In order to connect with someone, friend or enemy, the mystical key is to move beyond the level of argument to the silent rhythms that only the spirit perceives. Speak to someone in the silence of meditation. Speak there, in the holiness of the inner shrine from your most naked, loving truth. Hear there how his soul responds. It will. We are not bound by the physical level, unless we choose to be.

Where we love, let us deepen that love through silent communion in the chambers of the heart. Where we experience conflict, let us find the soul of the other in silence, in prayer. Let us release to God our lack of harmony and ask Him to heal the harsh and broken connection between us.

∾

Dear God,

I take into the holy temple, the sacred shrine within my heart, my relationship to this person.

I speak here in Your presence, dear God, my honest feelings and perception of the other.

Our connection is the most holy place, for it is the oneness between brothers.

Where we walk in harmony, may our harmony increase and cast a light over all the world.

Where we are lost in confusion and do not understand, then please, dear Lord, help us remember the Truth.

I open my heart to this person now.

I speak from my fear and my hurt and my pain,
  to You, dear Lord, and to the soul of my
  brother.

Let me hear him also.

Let me not be hardened to the truth of any
  heart.

Let me understand as I have not understood,

And see what I have not seen,

That we might both be freed from this tear in
  the holy fabric.

Where the fabric is rent, please enter me and
  reweave it.

Thank You, Lord.

In the silence and the sanctity of the time I
  spend with You, may my heart and inner eye
  be opened.

Amen.

SEX

Sex, like all things, is righteous to the extent that
heaven meets earth there. In modern times, the
physical drama of sex is overvalued, while its

spiritual meaning is underappreciated. We tend to overemphasize, to literally idolize sex, not because we appreciate its importance but because we do not. By cheapening sex, we fail to honor it. By casting a garish, ugly light upon its every detail, we hide our faces from its mystery.

Sex is not, in its essence, about the body at all. It is an opportunity for us to remove our emotional armor with someone who wants us to remove it and who wants to remove his or her own. Problems occur when we have sex with people who have no desire whatsoever for us to be so naked in their presence, who have no sense of the sacred responsibility it is to hold another person's heart in their hands.

Sex, when it is a vehicle for love, is holy. Sex without love is dangerous. It leads to pain and some level of emotional destruction, whether consciously experienced immediately or not. Sex should be a deepening of communication, not a substitute for it. Sex that is sacred is a marriage of hearts. In this fierce and fiery joining the beginning of the world is reenacted. Something is born whether we conceive or not, for we are chemically altered, profoundly changed by the act of having fully expressed ourselves and shared our love deeply.

It is one of our sicker cultural obscenities that we present sex to our children via media in such incredibly casual, loveless images. It is an area where the modern home is bombarded with darkness: Where sex is degraded, love is degraded; where love is degraded, the world falls apart.

When honesty, vulnerability and kindness form a backdrop to the emotional risk of the moment, sex is an experience of great light. Its healing power is legion. Great sex is emotional starlight. We have sex a million times in an effort to achieve that one in a million.

If we had over-the-moon sex on a regular basis, sex that rings from the soul and sends shockwaves through us, there would be less disease, less anger and probably less war. If every man and woman alive could feel the crazy, delirious rush of the soul when it touches the soul of another, this world would be a happier place. Our demeaning, gross and pathetic attempts to sexualize the world inappropriately—libidinizing products that we do not need in order to manufacture false desire to feed our commercial machinery—is an immorality. It lacks respect not only for human beings, but also for the role that sex can and should play in a spiritually mature existence.

Why do we as a culture sensationalize and exploit dark and meaningless sex? Because we lack the experience of its dazzling light. In failing to cultivate a healthy respect for sexual power, we become vulnerable to its misuse. Anything repressed expresses itself inappropriately. God celebrates pleasure; only people condemn it. A righteous experience of sex cannot be found outside a spiritual center, an authentic human soulfulness, because nothing can. That which is within us can save us, but the same things misused are the things that will destroy us.

There's a state of being that is raw and authentic and fiercely graceful, like a great ballerina dancing in her prime. Sex in that place is more than just sex. With every couple who make it past the sad disconnection of sex that's just sex to the fire at our center, the world is brought closer to the end of its pain. How excruciating to have touched that place, and then to land unsuspectingly back in the world as we knew it: the cold, nonintimate, unsoft world of people who cannot find each other. That's why we should never have sex casually. If you're not with a person who's an artist at love, the art of love is a dangerous game.

A lot of people can join us for the view of heaven that sex can give. But there aren't a lot of people who can stay awake in the morning, who have the personal skills to hold on to the vision once the sun has risen and the world is calling. It takes depth and maturity, or the innocence of youth, to have the personality structure it takes to cherish today whom we cherished last night.

So be careful but be brave—that's what the good witch of good sex would tell us. And God—what would He say? Oh, I think He would say, be careful but be brave. In your arms you are holding the most precious creature: my child in whom I am adoringly pleased. Love him and honor him, be kind to him and bring him deep peace. Pray that your energies might bless and protect him. Surrender your heart and surrender your soul.

Pray before, pray during, pray after.

Dear God,

May sex, like everything else, be in my life, or
    not in my life, according to Your will.

May it be an instrument of healing, of love and
    sacred power,

For me and anyone with whom I am joined.

May its spiritual secrets be revealed to me.

May all ugliness, cheapness, or loveless sexual
    thoughts and experience be cast out of my
    mind and body.

May God's spirit enter here.

May I do as You would have me do

And know what You would have me know

And have no experience of anything else.

May I never underestimate its power

Or the sacred responsibility that is placed in my
    hands when I so join with another.

May sex be only a sacred experience for me and
    any other with whom I am joined.

May I know its holiness and only that.

Thank You very much.

Amen.

There's a category of sex that is very dark. I mean rape, incest, molestation, abuse of any number of varieties, centered around sex, then lodged like a knife in people's souls. It is now more pervasive, more of an issue in American society, than anyone would have imagined or could have predicted twenty years ago. Millions of people are thought to carry the burden, the vicious psychic wounding of someone somewhere having violated them sexually. Sexual abuse survivors are haunted by horrible memories, in bed and out. Their efforts to forgive can feel like the need to lift a boulder with one little finger, their access to one of the most beautiful human energies having been sullied and damaged and grossly misused.

They are here among us and their tears run deep. This is not a joke. For every weak mind that makes up the story in therapy, there are thousands of others for whom the story is true, very painfully true.

Sexual abuse is an obscene betrayal. It is such a sign of the insanity of our times that anyone would touch a child, yet many people do; that anyone would rape, yet many people do; that anyone would have to suffer such a terrible degradation, yet many people have and do.

Dear God,
Please help me to heal the area of sex.
I feel so wounded, so damaged, betrayed by those
I thought were here to love me and protect me.
No words can say the pain I feel, when I
remember the abuse I suffered.
I surrender to You my memories and my anger
toward this person.
Please lift from me the burden of my resentment.
Please release me from this terrible pain.
Amen.

Dear God,
I release to You this terrible wound.
I surrender to You my pain, my anger, my fear
of disease, my feeling that I will never again
have a healthy experience of sex.

Only a miracle can lift this burden from my
   heart.
Please send Your angels to help me and heal me.
Help me feel my body is pure and not tainted.
Help me to forgive my offender, that peace
   might flood my heart.
Give me new life.
Thank You.
Amen.

⤫

(To be said by a healer)
In the name of God and all His angels, I cast
   out the demon left in you by this evil.
I say unto you, the force of darkness, be gone
   from this beloved child.
Through the power of God within us, I order
   you gone, nevermore to return or to cast your
   wicked energies in the direction of this pre-
   cious child of God.
In the name of God, I command you gone.
Dear God, please bind this prayer to earth.
Thank you very much.
Amen.

OBSESSION AND
ADDICTION IN LOVE

There are times when one person wants what another person doesn't. Who among us can't relate to the pain of an unrequited love and desire? It happens. When it does, we must remember that only an open heart will heal us; only our release of the other person, accepting them where they need to be, will stop the longing and set us free. Ask God to remove the obsession.

Fixation on another person can be as difficult and binding as an addiction to anything else. God can do for us what we cannot do for ourselves. Ask Him to deliver you both. It is not possible to achieve peace within ourselves while withholding love from another human being. We are released only from those whom we are willing to release.

❦

Dear God,
I am bonded in my heart to someone who does
   not share this bond.

I feel so drawn to (*name*), while she is not drawn
    to me.
Please, dear God, disconnect my heart from this
    longing within me that does not serve.
I release this person into Your hands.
May the ropes that bind my heart be cut.
May they not bind me.
May they not bind her.
I release her that I might be released.
Retract the silent hooks I have in her.
Bring back to me my power and my love.
Cut the cord that chemically ties me to her.
Free me from her.
Free her from me.
May we find peace.
Free us both.
Amen.

PRAYER FOR A
BROKEN RELATIONSHIP

Relationships are eternal; separation of our bodies does not mean separation of our souls. We are
healed by this knowledge because it reminds us

of the oneness of our relationship, regardless of the needs or conflicts that tear us apart.

Someone's leaving sometimes feels like the greatest pain we have ever suffered. But our relationships do not die, they just change form. Faith means knowing that no one is ever really gone.

~~~

Dear God,
In releasing this man, I surely feel as though my
    heart is crushed.
I feel as though a limb is gone, a piece of my
    self now ripped away.
I pray, dear God, for the power to love him so
    totally that I shall not be in pain.
For my love, I know, shall set me free.
Let me not be tempted to try to constrict him,
    either in my actions or in my thoughts.
May he fly free.
May I appreciate the rightness of his need to
    travel.
May I keep my faith in the wisdom of all
    things.
May I learn to respect his choices to go where
    he needs to go.

If he finds another love, may that love flourish,
  for Your sake.
For truly, the arc of love is a blessing on us all.
Wherever he goes, dear Lord, please go with
  him.
May he be blessed in all his doings.
Please protect him.
Bring him joy.
May he always be happy.
May he always be loved.
May he find his way.
Amen.

PRAYER FOR OUR HOME

Dear God,
May this house be a sacred dwelling for those
  who live here.
May those who visit feel the peace we have
  received from You.
May darkness not enter.
May the light of God shield this house from
  harm.
May the angels bring their peace here and use
  our home as a haven of light.

May all grow strong in this place of healing,
our sanctuary from the loudness of the
world.
May it so be used by You forever.
Amen.

PRAYER FOR OUR PARENTS

Dear God,
Please bless my parents.
Thank You, thank them for the life they gave
me.
For the ways they helped me and made me
strong, I give thanks.
For the ways they stumbled and held me back,
please help me to forgive them and receive
Your compensation.
May their spirits be blessed, their roads forward
made easy.
Please release them, and release me, from my
childhood now gone by.
Release us also from any bitterness I still hold.
They paved the way, in all that they did, for
where I have been has led me here.

I surrender my parents to the arms of God.

Thank you, dear ones, for your service to me.

Bless your souls.

May your spirits fly free.

May we enter into the relationship God wills
for us.

Thank You, Lord, for I am free now.

Glory, hallelujah.

Amen.

PRAYER FOR OUR CHILDREN

Dear God,

There are no words for the depth of our love
for this child.

We pray for her care and her protection.

We surrender her into Your hands.

Please, dear God, send Your angels to bless and
surround her always.

May she be protected from the darkness of our
times.

May she always see You at the center of her life.

May her heart grow strong,

To love You and serve You.

We surrender, dear God, our parenthood to You.

Make us the parents You want us to be.

Show us how to love most patiently, to be there
for her most fully,

To understand profoundly who she is and what
she needs.

May this family be a blessing unto her now and
forever.

May she learn here values and principles of love
and righteousness.

May she learn from us kindness.

May she learn from us strength.

May she learn from us the lessons of power:

That she has it,

That she must surrender it to You to be used
for Your purposes throughout her life

For thus shall You be gladdened,

And thus shall she be free,

To live most fully and love most deeply.

That is our wish.

That is our prayer for her and for us forever.

Amen.

PRAYER FOR MYSELF

Dearly beloved God,
In whom I lay my trust,
Please give me new life.
Fill every cell of my being, transform each
thought, cleanse every heartbeat,
That I might be as You would have me be.
Take away the darkness of my past.
Fill me with Your blessing and graciousness.
Allow me rebirth from the many deaths I have
endured in this life.
Dear God,
I have been through the wars.
Where I have been weak, please make me strong.
Where I perceive myself as guilty, please show
me my innocence.
Where I block my healing or full empowerment
or full experience of love and joy, please show
me my wound and take from me its sting.
May I experience the beauty, the abundance, the
power and the joy that is Your wish for all
mankind,
That I might be a vessel for these things in the
lives of others.

The wicked in myself and others has tormented
me.
Please cast away that darkness from my life.
I know Yours is the power,
I know Yours are the holy truths, the currents of
love and power that remain,
And so I ask, dear God, please remove the bur-
dens on my heart,
Cast out the demons from my mind and my
environs.
May I see the light at the center of my being.
I believe in Your power within me.
I know it is there.
Dear God, help me find it.
I have faith in Your light.
Please show it to me that I might give up the
fight to be anything other than who I am.
May I fly with angels and sing with angels and
know the angels in myself and others
Henceforth and forever as You have promised.
Please hold my hand.
Please take me home.
Please move me forward.
Thank You, Lord.
Amen.

6

Prayers for Work and Creativity

WORK

The love within us is meant to extend outward. The closer we grow to our inner light, the more we feel the natural urge to share that light with others. So it is that we all long for meaningful work, some creative endeavor that will be as our ministry, by which the energies within us might flow out to heal the world.

Our activity in the world is our work. Our primary work, as we have already established, is to love and forgive. Our secondary work is our worldly employment. The meaning of work, whatever its form, is that it be used to heal the world.

The essence of a business is the vision behind it, and illumined vision is service to humanity. Love is the most powerful fuel in any endeavor. The most important question to ask about any work is "How does this serve the world?" To whatever extent it contributes healing of some form to society, to that extent the project is blessed. Blessing means mystical support and protection. If you want your business to succeed, pray only that it serve mankind.

God doesn't love anyone over anyone else. There is no atom in the universe more blessed than any other. No one has more potential for greatness than anyone else. The ultimate success of your career will not be determined by credentials, backing, or marketing techniques. It will be determined by your ability to access the spiritual gulf stream. Prayer makes that happen. Prayer is our way of signing up with the army of light and receiving its reinforcements on a regular basis. The light is a realm of consciousness rising up around us, altering the dominant mental paradigm of our age. Its function is to replace the energies of selfishness with compassion, and competition with service, that we might cast out fear through the power of love. We pray that our talents and intelligence serve a higher cause than the fulfillment of our self-centered goals. Thus we access the purification process, a recovery from past mistakes that aligns us with integrity and delivers us to excellence.

Our prayer is that our excellence might come forth and serve the world. That is power. That is success. Winning at someone else's expense is an old paradigm and an increasingly obsolete model of success. Separation leads to disintegration, and joining leads to miracles.

❧

Dear God,
As I go to work today, may Your spirit go with
    me.
May my work in the world be a vehicle for your
    love.
May it fulfill a divine mission.
May it shine and light up all darkened places.
Go with me, Lord.
Show me how to love and forgive each person,
    that I might carry Your light to all I meet.

This is a new day, may it not be darkened by
   yesterday's unforgiveness.
Instead, dear Lord, may we begin anew with
   new strength, new creativity, new power, new
   love.
If I am the employer, make me kind and com-
   passionate.
Show me the art of leadership.
If I am the employee, make me kind and com-
   passionate.
Show me the art of service.
For we are all in Your service, Lord, and here to
   lead the earth out of darkness into light.
May our work do this, through Your power
   within us.
And so it is.
Amen.

Dear God,
Before I go to work today, please lift my mind
   to the realm of Truth.
May I remember and not forget throughout the
   day that my only work is to love, for

Your Sake, that the world might be renewed.

I think of my workplace—the people, the circumstances, the situations—and I surrender
them to you.

I remember, Lord, that this is but a veil across a
truer truth.

I withdraw my judgments, my interpretations,
my agendas.

I ask only to be a healing force.

This business is but a front for a temple, a healing place where people shall be lifted above
the insanity of a frightened world.

So may it be that I contribute to this healing, to
this upliftment, with my efforts and my
resources.

And that is all I ask.

Dear God,

Send Your angels to every person at my workplace, to every person who will come there
today and forever.

If I am tempted to judge or criticize anyone,
please heal me of my limited vision.

May I see only the truth.

May I work from integrity and excellence and
full force of Your power within me, that I

may know my true strength and contribute it
to this world.

May my presence at work be a blessing on others and on myself.

Thank you, Lord, for showing me the way now
and forever.

Thank You.

Amen.

❧

Dear God,

I dedicate this work to You.

Imprint Your mind upon it.

Fly with it unto the heavens.

Use it to shower Your love onto the world.

Thank you for Your faith in me that such a glorious mission has been placed in my hands.

Amen.

❧

Dear God,

I surrender to You my striving.

I let go all need to effort or to struggle.

I relax deeply into things exactly as they are.
I accept life, that it might move through me
    with grace.
Amen.

PRAYER FOR ACHIEVEMENT

Many times, we are held back by a sense that we
are simply not good enough, talented enough or
smart enough to do what we want to do. We pray
for God to free us from the internal chains that
bind us. Self-confidence stems from confidence
in Him. It is not we alone who do the work. The
work is done by Him who is within us.

Dear God,
I feel that my life is less than it should be.
I cannot find my freedom or my passion.
I have so much inside me that stays shut down,
    that isn't free.
I hurt so much to know I am not living at full
    force.

My talents are not used as I wish.

My abilities are not fully formed.

My energies are so suppressed.

Dear Lord, I do not know how to break free of the ways I constantly negate myself.

I hold myself prisoner somehow.

I know I do.

I know it is my own illusion, this prison in which I live, yet I cannot break free, though I try so hard.

Please, dear God, break down the walls that surround me.

Melt this prison.

Free my soul that I might be as You would have me be:

Free to live,

To soar,

To create,

To love,

To feel passion for good,

To do the good with passion.

I wish to fly.

I wish to feel Your full abundant spirit in me.

Give me this miracle.

Thank You.
Amen.

PRAYERS FOR DELIVERANCE

Dear God,
Deliver me to my passion.
Deliver me to my brilliance.
Deliver me to my intelligence.
Deliver me to my depth.
Deliver me to my nobility.
Deliver me to my beauty.
Deliver me to my power to heal.
Deliver me to You.
Amen.

Dear God,
I desire to help create a new context for human
    work and wealth, in which all people might
    prosper, in which all poverty might disappear,
    in which all of us might achieve as
You would have us achieve, and give to others as
    You would have us give.

Let the illusions that hold us back, dear God, as
individuals and as a society, now disappear.

Let me have new energy.

Let me have a new sense of purpose.

Let me know that I am on this earth to serve.

Let me not feel guilty about the expression of
my power,

Let me no longer play small, regardless of other
people's reactions to me when I play big.

I am willing to receive an expanded set of
options that You, dear God, might work miracles in my life, that You might cast out all
negative and limited conditions of this world.

May I receive a future unlike the past, for myself
and others.

For I now open my mind to possibilities I have
not dreamed of, to forces of life I have not
allowed in, and to realms of joy I have hardly
imagined.

I let go.

I release everything that blocks me in this
endeavor, from my past, from my present,
and from my future.

May I awaken from the dream of my inadequate
self.

Amen.

RELEASING OUTCOME

Dear God,

I release this business, project or goal to You.

I know that my tension, my control, and my
  direction do not serve the project or You.

May my resources be used by You.

I ask only that Your will be done.

I have shown up, Father,

I have done as I have felt You have asked me to
  do.

And now I place all outcome in Your hands.

May my efforts gladden You,

May my work please You.

I am here only to do Your bidding, that I might
  feel lighter, that I and the entire world might
  be healed.

Amen.

~∞~

Dear God,

May I have meaningful work and meaningful
  activity in my life.

I desire to wake up each morning and feel that I
  am used on behalf of something glorious.

I want to feel, no matter what my work, that I
dispense blessing, love, forgiveness, and kindness there to all I meet.

Help me to remember that You are the power.

May I not overglorify merchandizing or money
or business.

May my work be Yours.

May my work be love.

Help me to remember that as I focus on the
realm of heaven, everything else will take care
of itself.

Help me to have faith to know the universe
shall take care of me as I take care of it.

In this moment, I am willing to put aside all
small and worthless values.

In this moment, I am willing to let go my attachment to money, popularity, power, prestige,
the things of the world that I do not need.

For I know that they are all illusion, and except
as they are sent by You, they lead me
nowhere.

Thus shall I shine.

And as I shine and sparkle, I shall radiate a
power in this world, not of this world, and
people will not fail to notice.

For I shall be as a star in a darkened sky.
I shall go to sleep knowing that I did as I have
    come here to do.
I shall be repaid by gratitude, shining in the eyes
    of my brothers.
Please shine in my heart.
Amen.

TRANSFORMING FAILURE

Dear God,
There are times when Love's call seems entirely
    in vain, when all I can see around me is my
    failure.
I have not succeeded in the area of my heart's
    desire.
I do not seem to have the magic ingredient that
    enables some people to move forward in ways
    I cannot.
What is wrong with me?
Am I without blessing?
Dear God,
Please help me.
Restore to me my faith in who I am.

Give me aid.
Give me faith.
I give myself to You.
Amen.

PRAYER FOR NEW BEGINNINGS

Dear God,

I feel that I have wasted my life, thrown away
my resources, taken too much time to gather
my strengths.

Now, dear God, I feel it is too late for me.

My age, my weaknesses, the lies and betrayals of
time gone by, all make me seem a lesser tal-
ent.

And only You, dear God, know the love in my
heart and how much I want to serve, how
much I have to give.

I need a miracle, a new beginning, which only
You can give me.

Please, dear God, I give my life to You.

Please bring together my talents.

Please increase my gifts and use them for Your
purposes.

I surrender my future.
Make it unlike my past.
Thank You very much.
Amen.

MONEY

Money has inappropriately become the bottom line in today's society. It needn't be that way, for other things could be the bottom line instead: that people be happy, that children be cared for, that peace reign.

There is nothing wrong with money. Like everything else, it can be used for purposes of healing or purposes of destruction. It isn't evil to make money. We can be getting paid for a job and still not be doing it for the money.

When that is our attitude, in fact, we are at our most abundant. Internal abundance produces external abundance. Purity does not mean absence of cash. It means that you desire for money to be in your life to whatever extent and in whatever way it would serve God's purposes.

We must create a new context for the experience of wealth. What has been used to oppress can be used to heal. Seek us first the kingdom of heaven. . . .

⌘

Dear God,
I surrender to You my wealth, I surrender to
    You my debts.
Whatever fear I have about money, please
    remove this fear from my mind.
Whether I believe that money is scarce, or
    money is too important, or money is bad, or
    money is unspiritual, whatever my ideas are
    that block me—and You know what they
    are—dear Lord, please help me.
I wish to have whatever abundance You see fit
    for me.
I want money to flow freely into me and
    through me, that it might bless my life and
    the lives of others.
I surrender to You now any judgments I might
    have on those who have wealth.

I do not wish to judge, for I know my judgment
holds back my own abundance.

Whatever lack of integrity I might have shown,
if I am indebted or have violated anyone else,
please wash me clean and heal my mind.

I make amends to You and to this person in my
heart.

Please show me what behavior You would have
me follow, Lord, that I might begin again.

Please place within my mind the attitudes
toward money that You would have me hold.

I give up my own interpretations and ask for
Yours.

Whatever money comes to me, may it be used
to serve You.

Thank You very much.

Amen.

❧

I was recently seated at a dinner party next to the
CEO of a very large and successful clothing
company. "Your ads are wonderful," I told him.
"You're one of the few corporations in America

whose advertising actually contributes to our cultural life." As dinner went on, we were discussing with our hosts the various problems and challenges of being in business today. "Here's something you might try," I said to my new friend. "You could institute a policy whereby all of the employees in your company observe one minute of silence each morning, right before business hours begin. One minute of quiet reflection for world peace.

"First of all, it would have a wonderful effect on the country, because everybody would hear about it and it would set a fabulous example of *true* corporate responsibility. Also, I'm telling you, it would increase your profits because it would diminish extraneous, nonexcellent energy."

The country is literally falling apart from lack of wisdom, lack of centeredness, and lack of grace. We are so completely drunk on the cacophonous, hysterical stimulus of our popular culture we have little appreciation left for the sounds of genuine beauty, much less silence. Were the majority of Americans—at school, at homes, and in businesses—to take one minute each morning to commune together in silence, contemplating our higher power, this country would transform. The inner life is like a garden we haven't really thought of planting, which will bear all the fruit we could ever want, once we think to tend its needs.

· 7 ·

Prayers for the World

THE WORLD

There is no world outside us. The world is, in fact, our collective projections of love and fear, hopes and conflicts. In taking responsibility for our own thoughts and feelings, we play our part in the healing of the world.

The world is in a critical phase because we are. The world is in massive shift because we are. The world still has a chance for survival, both in spite of us and because of us.

Our prayers for the world are our greatest contribution to its healing and rebirth.

Dear God,

There is so much danger in the world today.

There is so much insanity, so much darkness
and fear.

Our human resources are not enough to counter
the evil on our streets and in our minds.

Dear God,

Please send a miracle.

Into every country and every home, into every
mind and every heart, may the power of Your
spirit now trigger the light, activate our holiness, remind us of the truth within.

May a great love now encompass us, a deep
peace give us solace.

For Lord, we live in fearful times, and we long
for a new world.

We surrender what is, to the bonfire of Your
genius.

Refine this metal.

Refashion our creations.

Remind us of the eternal truths.

Return to us our native grace.

Take back what we have kept and thus condemned.

For You are mighty, Lord, and can do what we
cannot.

May the world be reborn.

Help us forgive and leave the past behind us, the
future to be directed by You.

Hallelujah, for You have the power.

Praise and thanksgiving, for You use it to save
us, to heal us, to lift us from the past.

And we accept.

Thank You very much.

Amen.

THE HEALING OF NATIONS

On August 1, 1994, the Polish nation commem-
orated the fiftieth anniversary of the Warsaw
Uprising, in which 200,000 Poles were killed by
German Nazis, and 500,000 more were transported to concentration camps.

During this commemoration, German president Roman Herzog made an extraordinary
apology to the Polish people. "Today, I bow
down before the fighters of the Warsaw Uprising
as before all Polish victims of the war," he said.
"I ask for forgiveness for what has been done to

you by Germans. . . . It fills us Germans with shame that the name of our country and people will forever be associated with pain and suffering, which was inflicted on Poland a million times. We mourn the dead of the Warsaw Uprising and all people who lost their lives in World War II."

Polish president Lech Wałeşa had invited the German president to take part in commemorative ceremonies as an "act of healing." He said, "We do not give absolution to the murderers in Warsaw, but we do not pass those feelings upon the German nation. . . . Blood and hatred are a curse of the twentieth century; may they disappear in the past along with it."

A sincere amends releases God's corrective energy within the giver as well as the receiver. The German nation will be as blessed by Herzog's apology, as will the Poles, who, as one Polish woman said, "had been waiting fifty years to hear this." The day after Herzog's speech, I read an editorial in an American newspaper in which Herzog's apology was lauded. "Now," said the American newspaper editor, "if only the Japanese would do the same toward the Chinese!" Oh, please. The United States has its own profound apologies to make.

The expansion of this country was accomplished at the cost of decimation to the Native American population. The American Indian death toll due to the United States' march to the Pacific was massive. Much of the land we stole from the Native Americans is uninhabited to this day; basically, the Indians could have stayed where they were. Had America expanded its boundaries yet been true to its conscience, the American Indian nations could have remained intact. And were there a greater prevalence of Native American philosophy and culture in the United States today, the life of our nation would be immeasurably enriched.

While America has been a blessing on so many, we must not ignore our violations where they have occurred. The history of the African-American, also, is so morally outrageous as to make the fact that there has never been an official apology almost unbelievable. A strange psychological phenomenon occurs when a truth is so big, so obvious, that it becomes, in some perverse way, almost easy to resist. The history of racism in the United States is so cruel yet systemic in our society. Perhaps we fear we could not bear the feelings of guilt that would be unleashed were we to make to African-Americans a sincere and heartfelt amends. The truth is it is not our guilt that would be unleashed but our love. Making a formal apology to African-Americans is what we need to do in order to morally resurrect as a nation. In our hearts, white America needs to make an amends to the Native American and to the African-American, at least as much as they need to hear it. The miraculous powers of healing and correction that would be released were we to do so would be medicine for our nation's soul. What President Herzog did for the Germans, we can do for ourselves.

Admitting when we have been wrong is not a sign of weakness but one of strength. In situations where the people responsible for the perpetration of violence or violation are not even *alive* anymore, it should be that much easier for us to sincerely express regret, ask for forgiveness, and allow the love of God to reconcile us with our brothers.

Many people think that we have done enough to repay black America for the ravages of racism. The truth is that we have done far too little, for we have never apologized. We have never fully, publicly acknowledged the evil that was done to African-Americans *as* evil. The Civil War obliterated a wicked institution, but a war alone cannot obliterate wicked thinking. Slavery ended but racism continued, and in many ways it intensified after that war. Slavery existed only in the South, but racism pervades the entire country.

Only moral regeneration can restore this nation or any other. A sincere apology goes far toward restoring a genuine moral order, for it realigns basic energies with truth. Many people register the need for forgiveness while underestimating the importance of an apology. To ask someone to forgive you without actually apologizing is bogus and callous and patronizing.

Beneath every political wound is a personal one, and personal wounds must be addressed on a personal level. The power of God is medicinal. Other means can treat our wounds but only a spiritual experience can *heal* them. Forgiveness heals our souls by washing us clean of the past and delivering us to an unsoiled present. Eternity means a present untainted by past pain or future anxiety. Anything short of a spiritual healing can suppress the past but cannot erase it.

In America today, racial disharmony increases with every generation. With each generation more and more cellular memories are added onto the pile, resulting in rage and anger that cannot be politically contained. Hatred cannot be controlled; it must be undone. This, only God can do. As President Herzog assured his hosts in Warsaw that he understood the anger of Poles but begged for forgiveness in order that the future might be made new, so must we, as Americans, ask forgiveness from those whom we have violated in order that we might release both past and future into the hands of God.

There is a charismatic Catholic priest named Father DiOrio, who is known for his power as a faith healer. I attended one of his services, in which he had all Catholics say to non-Catholics, "If I or any of my people have ever done anything to offend you or your people, please forgive me and please forgive us." As a Jew, experiencing that request for forgiveness was one of the most profound experiences of my life—and I wasn't even consciously aware of my anger. I was thoroughly surprised by the tears that ran down my cheeks on receiving that apology for my people. I felt that I was literally standing in for my ancestors in that moment. I know firsthand what the making of a group amends can do.

In various cities throughout the United States, I have led the following ritualized apologies to the African-American and Native American peoples. They represent their forefathers as well as their children's children, as they participate with us in embracing God's Answer to the pain of a wrongful past.

Like Father DiOrio, I have asked African-Americans and Native Americans to stand, then hold the hands of a white American next to them.

Repeating after me, white America then says:

AMENDS TO THE AFRICAN-AMERICAN

To the African-American of the United States:
For what has been done to hurt you and offend
    you,
For the evils of racism throughout our history,
Please forgive me and please forgive this country.
I acknowledge to you the evils that have
    occurred here

In your life and in the lives of your ancestors.
On behalf of my nation, I deeply apologize.
If I could rewrite history I would, but I cannot.
God can. Dear God, please do.
I acknowledge now the genius of your people,
And the brilliance of your spirit,
And the pain you have endured.
May the demon of racism be cast off,
Out of this country and away from this world.
May there be in this nation a correction and
    resurrection,
That nevermore shall any hearts be enslaved.
May the future be made new,
May the pain of the past be gone forever.
May past hatred, dear God, now become a
    present love.
May forgiveness truly wash us clean.
May black and white America have a miraculous
    healing.
May we begin again as brothers, for that is what
    we are.
God bless your children unto all generations.
May the spirit of this amends bring peace to
    your soul. Truly, you have waited long.
I bless your children.

Please bless mine.
I thank you.
And I thank God.
Amen.

AMENDS TO THE
NATIVE AMERICAN

To the nations of the Native American Indians,
    as a citizen of the United States I say, please
    forgive me and please forgive us.
On behalf of my ancestors and the group con-
    science of all America, I deeply apologize for
    the wrongs, so cruel, that have been inflicted
    upon your people.
So many lives lost, yet still they haunt the psy-
    che of all people of goodwill,
We ask that the spirit of God give us absolution.
We as a nation have wronged.
Now we as a nation make amends.
How sorry we are for the suffering of your
    people.
If we could rewrite history, we would.
We cannot, but God can.

May history begin again.

May the spirit of your people now be reborn.

For we embrace and honor the spirit of the
Native American tribes.

We bless and commit to the good of your children and your children's children.

May we begin anew.

May your star rise high in the sky of this nation
and all others.

May the wrongs of the past now be made right
that your nation might be blessed, that our
nation might be blessed.

So be it.

Please, God, make these things right in love, in
healing, in mercy, in grace.

Amen.

HATRED IN AMERICA

The source of violence is in our heads. As it
would not be appropriate to ignore "just a little"
cancer in the body, so it is not appropriate for us
to ignore "just a little" violent thinking. A little
cancer, unchecked, turns into a monstrous killer.

So do small, insidious, seemingly harmless judgmental thought forms become the pervasive can-
cers that threaten to destroy a society.

As the body's defenses against cancer center
around a healthy immune system, our chief
defense against violence in America is our own
individual efforts to cleanse our minds of violent
thinking. Each and every one of us tends to be
angrier and less tolerant of others than we know
in our hearts that we should be. A healthy, civi-
lized society can absorb some anger and dysfunction, as a healthy immune system can absorb
some disease. But a massive buildup of anger and
mean-spiritedness bombarding our social system
day in and day out in millions upon millions of
individual doses overwhelms our societal defenses.
Medicine does little good in the absence of a
healthy immune system. Likewise police and
other institutional efforts to counter violence do
little good, ultimately, in the absence of our individual efforts to deal with it. Violence is routed
out of the world only by being routed out of our
minds. Hatred is diseased thinking. Just as a cancer cell was a healthy cell that then transformed,
so is hatred, love gone wrong. In the areas of

both mind and body, we must think more in terms of cultivating health rather than always waiting for the time in which we inevitably must fight disease. Each of us is a cell in the social body. Whether we are a malignant or a healing force is up to each of us on a moment by moment basis. With every thought, we decide whether to be a cancer cell or a healthy immune cell, whether to give in to the tendency to place blame on others or to be a vehicle for God's love and forgiveness. Either we clean up the anger, or the anger will overwhelm us.

The only thing we can be one hundred percent responsible for is our own minds. The recognition that this is indeed quite a lot must now break through into mass awareness. In the United States today, there is a widespread, malignant thought form that *other people are the problem.* Conservatives tend to blame liberals for our problems, while liberals blame conservatives. The media blames almost everyone, and almost everyone blames immigrants. Some people are convinced homosexuals are the problem, while others think that single mothers are the problem. Still others think the Christian Right is the problem, and far, far too many people think that our parents were the problem. The entire culture has become a hysterical blame session.

Yet a healthy, vital society is not one in which we all agree. It is one in which those who disagree can do so with honor and respect for other peoples' opinions, and an appreciation of our shared humanity. Without personal commitment to the attributes of fair play and integrity, the United States is in grave danger. Malice and intolerance stalk our society, staking claim to our minds, and not one corner of our social order is unaffected. This darkness is a significant threat to our national good, perhaps the most significant threat in our history, for it strikes at the heart of democracy. Where people are not free to disagree, there can be no democracy, since that is what democracy *is.*

Hitler could never have risen to power had it not been for vast numbers of people who gave him that power. Although they did not share his hatred, they did not have a solid, moral commitment to *not hate.* Only a society in which there is a widespread commitment to *not hate* is safe from hatred. A little hatred is like a little cancer. And who among us does not hate?

The only way to protect our freedom is to check the hatred in our own minds. Our political conversation must shift away from the mass, infantile finger-pointing that now pervades it. It is not liberals *or* conservatives who have ruined or are ruining America; it is the tendency on so many people's parts to think that their way is the right way and that people who disagree with them are *bad*. It doesn't ultimately matter so much how we degenerated into such mass disrespect for the rights of others to hold opinions different from our own. What does matter is that we commit, immediately, to individual healing, through the grace of God, from our own tendency to condemn whom God Himself would not condemn. God loves Bill Clinton and Rush Limbaugh both, and He loves them equally. He sees through their politics, and He asks us to do the same. That might be a bitter pill for some people to swallow; it's the only medicine which will heal us, however, for it is a return to a spiritually healthy ground of being.

God does not need us to condemn each other on His behalf, but to love each other on His behalf. From that awareness, we can disagree vehemently yet appropriately. Disagreement must be respectful, or the disrespect itself poisons us more than either side's position in the argument ever could. Our freedom is ultimately not guaranteed by the constitution; the only thing that guarantees freedom, ultimately, is our own commitment to it. That commitment must include our capacity to love each other as human beings, to remember we are brothers on this planet, and to surrender to God any thoughts we have to the contrary. Let us not be deceived. Each of us is host to anger each day, just as each of us is host to love. Pray for your friends, but by all means pray for your enemies. And don't pray that they'll change; pray that *you* might change, from an accusatory mind to a loving one.

Without a spiritual basis, every system disintegrates. Any branch that does not bear fruit will fall off the tree. We mustn't think America is immune to the viruses that destroy nations, any more than any of us are immune to the flu if it's coming through town. Many of the things that most of us were brought up to think "could never happen here," have already begun to happen: dangerous scapegoating, violent hate crimes, small-minded intolerance for the views of others.

At what point are symptoms seen as signs of critical disease? And at what point do we wake up enough to know that without treatment this disease will destroy us? It is more important that we renew dignified and respectful dialogue with those who do not agree with us than that we keep slavishly congratulating those who have the wisdom to see things our way.

Within each of us lies the disease, and within each of us lies the divine physician. We must pray to Him, to be healed and made whole.

∽༄∼

Dear God,
Please remove from my mind the tendency to
    judge.
Please remove from my mind the tendency to
    hate.
Please remove from my mind the tendency to
    blame.
Please reveal to me, Lord, a way to stand in my
    power, through love instead of fear, and
    through peace instead of violence.

May I hear not the voice for anger, but only the
    voice for love.

And teach me, dear Lord, how not to hate those
    who hate me.

Transform all darkness into light, dear God,

And use my mind as an instrument of Your
    harmlessness.

I surrender to You my thoughts of violence.

Take these thoughts, Lord, and wash them
    clean.

Thank You very much.

Amen.

HEALING AMERICA

There's an odd way in which the United States
has begun to turn its back on some of the cor-
nerstone principles of our founding. From the
inception of our country, it has been a mainstay
of American consciousness that the fabric of our
nation would be woven from the threads of myriad national and ethnic identities. We would be
the melting pot of all nations. The vast majority
of Americans are descendants of immigrants, yet

we often act as though today's immigrants don't deserve what we do, that we have something to protect from their encroachment. It seems paradoxical to me that we would brag about our ancestors' coming over on the Mayflower, yet condemn someone trying to do the same thing today.

Of course there are immigrants who abuse our system, just as there are people born here who abuse our system. The truth is that the majority of today's immigrants bring with them an infusion of the same values that our ancestors personified, the values America is so sorely lacking. They are people willing to work hard for long hours to make a better life for themselves and their families. Our children do not stand to be corrupted by their values, so much as their children stand to be corrupted by ours. The scapegoating of today's immigrants makes a mockery of the American dream. It is a national immorality when we collectively say no to compassion.

Compassion need not, indeed should not, be considered synonymous with profligate financial expenditure. It means simply a mental commitment to accept the possibility of options we had theretofore not considered. Faith does not cost money. Love does not cost money. Throwing money at a problem, it is true, is not always the answer. But throwing love at a problem always is.

Jesus had only a few fish, but many more materialized. He had only a few loaves, but many more appeared. Where love is present, miracles happen. Where the consciousness of God is present—the desire and willingness to love—there God is, for He is invoked through our willingness to serve His children. Commitment to love produces expanded possibilities. As long as our minds are aligned with His love, the physical world will support our desires. There is certainly a difference between love and enabling, but there is also a difference between taking care of ourselves and selfishness. The universe will not support our selfishness, for it is not of God. The closing of the American heart is the greatest threat to our national good.

I know a woman who was about to marry a man with two children from a former marriage. She said to me, "I don't want to be just a tolerant stepmother; I want to be an *embracing* stepmother." She told me that she had prayed to God and asked Him to remove any barriers she still

had to truly letting the stepchildren into her
heart. In America today, many remind us, "We
must have tolerance." But actually, tolerance is
not enough. We must have love. We must ask
God to remove from our hearts any feelings that
we are superior to anyone, or that we should have
more rights to opportunity than anyone else. For
there is no private good, in the end. We will all
have room here, or none of us will have room
here. Life is forcing us to manifest on earth the
consciousness of Heaven.

The history of the world proves that where
the haves do not share with the have-nots, the
have-nots always rise up. And when the have-nots
in turn become the haves, they either share with
the new have-nots or not. We who are the descendants of those who had not, yet through the
grace of God rose up to new life for themselves
and their children, must now recognize our challenges and divine responsibilities. As children of
God and as descendants of early Americans, we
must do unto others as we would have others do
unto us. We must love one another. *That* is morality; *that* is God's law.

Americans have a tendency to moralize, to say
endless things to other nations about how *they*

should clean up their houses. Surely we must clean up ours. The days are long gone when we had the genuine moral authority from which to preach to others. Let us regain that ground, take a fearless moral inventory, do the work on ourselves that we still need to do. It will heal our hearts and free our souls. There is new life waiting to happen here, as soon as we own up.

Nothing less will heal America.

PRAYER FOR AMERICA

Dear God,
We join in prayer to celebrate this nation and
    surrender its destiny to You.
We give thanks in our hearts for the founding
    of this country.
We give thanks for and bless the souls of those
    who came before us to found this nation, to
    nurture and to save it.
We ask that God's spirit now fill our hearts
    with righteousness.
May we play our parts in the healing and the
    furtherance of our country.

May we be cleansed of all destructive thoughts.

May judgment of others, bigotry, racism, and
intolerance be washed clean from our hearts.

May our minds be filled with the thoughts of
God,

His unconditional love and His acceptance of
all people.

May this nation be forgiven its transgressions,
against the African-American, Native
American, and any and all others.

May our lives be turned into instruments of
resurrection, that the sins of our fathers
might be reversed through us.

May the beauty and the greatness of this land
burst forth once more in the hearts of its
people.

May the dreams of our forefathers be realized
in us, that we might live in honesty and
integrity and excellence with our neighbors.

May this country once again become a light
unto the nations of hope and goodness and
peace and freedom.

May violence and darkness be cast out of our
midst.

May hatred no longer find fertile ground in
which to grow here.

May all of us feel God's grace upon us.

Reignite, dear God, the spirit of truth in our
hearts.

May our nation be given a new light, the sacred
fire that once shone so bright from shore to
shore.

May we be repaired.

May we be forgiven.

May our children be blessed.

May we be renewed.

Dear God, please bless America.

Amen.

AMENDS BETWEEN
MEN AND WOMEN

Prayers of forgiveness work on the personal level
as well as politically and socially.

Mutual forgiveness is the key to healing
between men and women. Until we have healed
the bitterness and misunderstanding that still
underlie the relationship between the sexes, we
will continue to project our conflicts onto the
canvas of the larger world.

꧂

(*Men to women*)

If I or any other man has ever done anything to
   hurt you or offend you, and for the manifold
   transgressions against women, you and every
   other, I apologize.

Please forgive me and please forgive us.

If you have ever felt demeaned, uncherished, or
   your womanhood betrayed in any way;

If I or any other man has failed to see the
   light of your sex and the brilliance of your
   female spirit, on behalf of all of us, I am
   so sorry.

May the beauty of women and the power of
   women and the vision of women now burst
   forth in our world and in our consciousness.

May the mind of man be healed.

May the heart of woman repair.

I commit to you and to God that I am, and
   shall be, a man who sees your value.

I see your light.

God bless you and your sisters, our mothers and
   our daughters.

I shall teach my sons to honor you.

May we never go back.
Amen.

⚬~⚬

(*Women to men*)

If I or any member of my sex has ever done
anything to hurt you or offend you or any
man, please forgive me and please forgive us.

If your life as a man has been stunted or
thwarted by any woman, I now stand in her
stead and apologize for me, for her, for all
womankind.

May God give us a healed vision of what it
means to be a man.

May men receive this healing.

May women receive this healing.

May we see your strength.

May we not emasculate.

May we honor your power and respect your
mind.

I shall teach my daughters well.

May your past be healed, your future made new
and strong.

May you reach your fullest joy.

Go with my love, and the love of all women,
    forever.
Amen.

PRAYER FOR THE LEADERS

We are experiencing a crisis of leadership now,
not so much because people lack the qualities necessary for it, but because we systemically invalidate
such qualities. It is hard in today's world for a person to stand up in excellence and power within the
public realm. There are myriad forces marshaled
against doing so, causing a massive brain and
spirit drain from the realms of worldly power.

Let us support the possibility of greatness, in
anyone at any time. We must rethink our attitudes about leaders, or at the rate we're going we
will soon have none. We must create the fertile
ground for leadership in order to prepare the way
for great leaders.

A politician listens to his or her constituents;
a leader listens to whispers in the wind.

Dear Lord,

We pray for the leaders of this country and every other.

May they not be swayed by politics but listen instead to the spirit of truth.

May they not harken to the false and bitter voices of a frightened world, but instead hear the angels who minister unto them.

May the world make room for their leadership and resist no more their growth into greatness.

May their virtue shield them.

May their lack of virtue be forgiven and corrected.

May their words be true.

May their strength go before them, to cut like a sword through all illusion.

May they see the innocence and brotherhood in those who oppose them.

May they grow beyond a shallow fight.

And thus may we all be taken with them into new light, new peace, new politics, new hope for all the world.

Amen.

The healer, in whatever form, is the priest who carries us back to the light. The transformers of the world, working with millions of people to heal their life energies, need mighty power to align with them in order to bring forth the enlightened society. Therapists, ministers, rabbis, priests, teachers, healers—there is an emerging healer consciousness in the world today, as we strive to make it to the light in time.

⤬

Dear God,
I surrender this session to You.
I ask that my interaction with this person be
   used for Your purposes.
I surrender all worldly thought I would bring
   from my past and ask, in this moment, to be
   filled with Your wisdom.
May I be used as a channel for Your healing
   power, for by myself I can heal no one.
Rather I remember that Your power within me
   does the work.

Show me how to love this person and listen to
him and counsel him as You would have me
do.
May I remind him of his own magnificence that
through this memory he might awaken to
truth.
May I minister to him truly through Your words
and Your thoughts and Your love.
Amen.

PRAYER FOR THE
VICTIM OF VIOLENCE

Dear God,
I have been abused and it has wounded my soul.
My memories, my thoughts, dear Lord,
Are full of horror,
And I am powerless to heal them.
The hatred I feel,
The pain I feel,
Is beyond my ability to deal with.
Please, dear God,
Come into my mind.
With your spirit, dear God,

Please wash me clean.
Take out of me this sword,
Take out of me this wound,
Take out of me this pain.
Help me forgive,
For it is beyond my power to do so myself.
Release the one who did this,
And release, dear God, my heart.
I need new life.
Please give me this.
Thank you, Lord.
Amen.

PRAYER FOR
THE PERPETRATOR

While we strive to heal the world, the darkness is putting up a massive assault on the planet. God's healing must extend itself, not to heal light but to heal the darkness.

The perpetrator of violence may or may not be consciously horrified by his own behavior. For those who are, that horror does not always lead to the cessation of criminal behavior. As with any addictive pattern where the drive toward certain behavior overwhelms and drowns the yearning of a human conscience, it is only through the power of a genuine spiritual awakening that the deepest darkness is turned to light.

For the perpetrator of wrong action, the need for prayer is great indeed. God hears all prayers. He judges no one.

⤜⤏

Dear God,
I recognize the evil of my behavior.
I ask forgiveness for the pain I've caused someone else.
Forgive me, God, and cleanse my heart.
Most of all, dear Lord, please send Your angels
    to release me from any yearnings to do again
    as I have done.
May God cast out this evil from within me.
May I be returned somehow, through Your
    grace, dear God, to the ways of goodness.
Please bless and protect those who have been
    victims of my perpetration.
May my life be somehow lifted up that I might
    be redeemed and receive from You the chance

to live the rest of my life on the path of
good, through the grace of God and in service to humanity forever and forever.
Amen.

PRAYER FOR THE EARTH

Dear God,
Please bless and protect this sacred jewel,
Our vulnerable planet so besieged.
May the rivers and the oceans and the sky and
   the land
All be repaired somehow, dear Lord.
May the barbarism end, which threatens to
   destroy our priceless treasure.
For surely the earth has been our home,
The home of our parents unto all generations.
For the sake of our children, Lord,
Save this earth.
Place in all minds a greater awe before her
   mysteries.
Shield her and heal her wounds,
Restore her to her former glory.
Save her, Lord, from us.
Amen.

And so it is that we pray with all our hearts and souls, to deliver our world into the hands of God.

⚬⚬

Dear God,
We pray for this our world.
We ask that You remove the walls that separate us and the chains that hold us down.
Use us to create a new world on earth, one that reflects Your will, Your vision, Your peace.
In this moment, we recognize the power You have given us to create anew the world we want.
Today's world, dear Lord, but reflects our past confusion.
Now, in this moment, we ask for new light.
Illumine our minds.
Use us, dear Lord, as never before, as part of a great and mighty plan for the healing of this world.
May we no longer be at war with each other.
May we no longer be at war within ourselves.

Let us forgive this century and every other, the
   evils of history, the pain of our common
   fears.
Remove from our hearts the illusion that we are
   separate.
May every nation and every people and every
   color and every religion find at last the one
   heartbeat we share,
Through You, our common Father/Mother and
   the redeemer of our broken dreams.
May we not hold on to yesterday.
May we not obscure Your vision of tomorrow
   but rather may You flood our hearts.
Flow through us, work through us, that in our
   lives we might see the illuminated world.
Create, sustain that world on earth, dear God,
   for us and for our children.
Hallelujah, at the thought,
Praise God, the possibility that such a thing
   could come to be, through You, through
Your light that shines within us.
So may it be.
So may it be.
We thank You, Lord.
Amen.

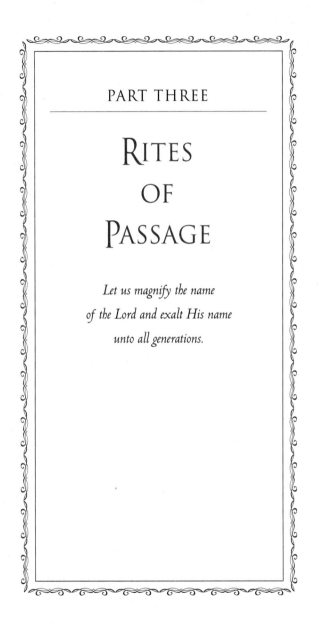

PART THREE

RITES
OF
PASSAGE

*Let us magnify the name
of the Lord and exalt His name
unto all generations.*

1

Ceremonies of Light

Rites of passage provide structures of energy by which we alchemize our experiences of the most significant junctures in life. They fortify our spirits, that nobility and transcendence might be more than just words. They remind us of our oneness and form society's connective tissue. As extensions of prayer, they are words that take us beyond words.

Most people in modern, secularized society have little or no experience of the positive value of rituals. Fleeing from the empty feelings of rigid, formalized ceremonies, we have thrown away the baby with the bathwater. Trying to make them more meaningful, we have often taken casualness to the point of meaninglessness, as lacking in substance as the uptight formality we sought to replace. Let us create anew the rituals of ancient significance, with respect for ideas that have borne the tests of time and openness to new ideas that reflect the needs of our own era. Our modern experience and any maturity we have gained give us the wisdom to go back to ceremonial rites and the courage, when helpful, to do them somewhat differently.

We are not the be-all and end-all of all generations. We are discovering the many ways in which we are not as smart as we thought we were, and part of our illumination is the humbling that comes from that realization. Some things do not change. There are spiritual traditions on the planet that know infinitely more, not less, than we do about the human heart. Yet we too must make our own mark upon the eternal march of ideas. A modern contribution means *our* contribution. In every area of human society, we must carve out transcendent ideals. Our mark so far has been that they are all but absent among us.

The following rites of passage offer ideas for blessing newborns, puberty rites, marriage, elder wisdom, divorce, and memorial services. These rites are not in any way meant to be set formulae or prescriptions. Use the ideas, play with them, add to them, make your own lasagna.

2

Blessing of the Newborn

(See also *Prayer for Our Children*)

OFFICIANT   We gather on this day, with this man and woman and their newborn daughter, to celebrate her entrance into the world. We are here to welcome her and pray for her. You have all been invited here because, as family and closest friends, your prayers and future involvement in the life of this child are requested by the mother and the father and blessed by God Himself. We join our thoughts and sincere goodwill, asking that a mantle of peace might embrace this family and an arc of God's light surround this child for all her days.

We are adults. We realize that the world is not now the place that it should be, that it does not vibrate with the name of the Father, with the love and light that He intends for all of us. For this reason, the birth of this child increases in us the intention and commitment to heal the world for her sake and prepare her well for the days ahead.

I would like to ask the grandparents of this child to join with me now, and repeat this prayer of blessing and protection:

Dear God,
Thank you for the birth of this beautiful child
    into the world and into this family.
We offer ourselves this day as caretakers of her
    spirit and her higher mind.
May we fulfill with strength the glory of our
    role, in her life and the lives of her parents.
May the spirit of this family, from generations
    past and into the future, burst forth to bless
    and protect this child.
Amen.

I would now like to ask that each grandparent say for all of us to hear, your hopes and wishes for this child and her life:

(The grandparents do.)

I would now like the godparents of this child to please come up here.

(The godparents hold the baby, and the parents step back.)
I remind you that you have been given an important task. It is with utmost gratitude and trust that this child's parents ask you to play this role. God Himself shall place within you the wisdom and the strength you need to hold within your minds forever the good of this child and the importance of the emotional responsibility now entrusted to you. Please express your commitment and wishes for this child:

(The godparents do.)
And now, to the parents: I would like to ask you to hold your child and receive our blessing.

Dear Lord,
We join together on this day, and pray for the
    life and well-being of this glorious child.
With her parents, we thank you for her entrance
    into this world.
With them also, we surrender this family, and
    invite God's spirit to enter here.
We pray for this couple, and ask that they be
    filled as parents with the spirit of the Lord.

May they receive Your strength with which to
   hold this child, Your love with which to raise
   her, and Your grace by which to guide this
   family now and forever.

   (*To the parents*)

What do you choose to name this child?

   (*The parents respond.*)

So be it. It is with faith and hope that we now
   name this child (*name*), daughter of (*name*)
   and (*name*), granddaughter of (*name*) and
   (*name*), (*name*) and (*name*).

   In the name of God and of generations before
and after us, we welcome you, dear child, to the
mystical union of souls on earth. We have
awaited you. We rejoice that you are here.

   We ask You, dear God, to bless her and protect her, now and forever.

   (*To the parents*)

Please repeat after me:

Thank You, God, for the birth of our daughter.
May she receive the gifts of grace this day.
We dedicate her life to You, that she may
   grow in love to become a woman strong
   and wise.

May we be the father and mother that You
would have us be.

Give us patience and wisdom.

Help us, Lord, to live in Your light.

May our home be blessed and guided by Your
will.

Thank You for Your faith in us that such a glorious child has been placed in our hands.

May she always remember her Father in Heaven.

May she never forget, throughout her life, that
You are her Source, that You are the Lord.

May she learn from us happiness; may she learn
from You everything.

Thank You, dear God.

Amen.

Will those gathered here please join with me now
in two minutes of silent prayer for this precious
child who has joined our midst.

   (*They do so.*)

And now, to you, the parents, I say on behalf of
all of us, go in peace and build a strong and
beautiful family life. Your wishes are rooted in
truth, for we have prayed with you and joined
our hearts with yours. Your prayers are our

prayers, that you might have a home that is full of love and righteousness for you and for your child. May she grow up to reflect the best in both of you and extend unto the world she touches the love she receives from her mother and father. Do not fear, for God will guide you always. Do not despair, for He is ever there. You are loved and you are cared for. The spirit of God is with you always, to guide you both and bless your children.

And so it is.

God bless you.

Amen.

3

Rite of Puberty:
The Consecration of Adulthood

Coming-of-age ceremonies provide a transitional context for the passage from girlhood to young womanhood and boyhood to young manhood. They ritualistically remind the young person, the family, and their community of the significance of this juncture.

OFFICIANT We are gathered here together to celebrate the entrance into young manhood of this beloved child of God, John.

John, on this day you are charged by God to enter formally with us into the adult population of the world. You have lived for thirteen years;

now you come to the final stages of your child-hood. Although we do not offer you a perfect world, we invite you now to participate with us fully in the sacred task of healing it and making it whole.

From this day forward, with our blessing and support, you shall receive the arc of your own destiny. You shall be full director, with God, of its movement through your life.

CONSECRANT   I, John, now stand before you, having lived thirteen years. Now, in full con-sciousness, I dedicate the rest of my life to the spirit of God and His purposes on earth.

GATHERING *(In unison)* May your days be blessed.
   Stand forth.
   Come forward.

CONSECRANT   I am an *(nationality)* *(religion)* *(eth-nic background)* *(sex)** and draw strength from those who came before me.

*What to include should be decided by the consecrant.

I honor you, the community of my elders, for what you have done and have not done to make the world I inherit a place of peace and love.

GATHERING *(In unison)*   We thank you.

CONSECRANT   I forgive you, the community of my elders, for what you have done and have not done to make the world I inherit a place of broken dreams.

GATHERING *(In unison)*   We thank you.
We apologize to you and to your generation for what we have done and what we have not done.

OFFICIANT   John, with this ceremony you take on the yoke of citizenship, full and now complete, in the spiritual community of this nation.

May you know in your life the joys of full and abundant manhood. May the world honor you for who you are.

Wherever you go, our blessings go with you. Whatever you do, may you find guidance and support. May you always consider us your loving friends.

(*The consecrant now delivers into the hands of the two most significant adults in his life [ideally, of course, his parents], some symbolic gift of his choosing, the material nature of which should not exceed the simplicity of this ceremony.*)

CONSECRANT   Thank you for all you have given me in raising me to this point. May God's rays shine on you always. Please release me now, as I release you, that I might find my manhood. May you be freed from the burdens of my childhood, as I am now freed. Please remain with me in guidance and support. May we enter into a new relationship now with each other and with ourselves.

You have earned my respect. You have earned my love. Thank you both. God bless you.

OFFICIANT   Now I say to the parents of this young man: This child shall be a child no longer. He enters now the adult world. (*For a boy:*) Free him and respect his choices. (*For a girl:*) Free her yet always cherish her heart. Pray always to God for the perfect attitudes and strengths by which to parent him now and prepare him further.

Do you now free him, that he shall be seen as a man in your eyes and ours and God's?

PARENTS   We do.

OFFICIANT   God bless you and thank you for the roles you have played in preparing this child to become a man. May the joys you have known as the parents of a child be replaced in full measure by the joys of being parents to a man.

And now, please share with us your wishes for your son.

(Both adults now share a message of hope and love and encouragement, written by them.)

OFFICIANT   Dear God, please bless this beautiful young man.

May the prayers of those who have loved him and raised him fill him up as he now goes forth. May he always be aware of his innocent nature. May angels surround him and uphold him all his days, henceforth and forevermore.

Young man, please state your intention to this gathering:

(The consecrant now declares a short message of planetary intention: to heal the world, to work on behalf of humanity's progress, etc. The consecrant will have sought the aid of whatever teachers or friends he wishes, to help

*him arrive at his message. Upon the completion of the
consecrant's message, the officiant continues.)*

And so it is. The adult community gathered here,
in representation of this nation and this world,
now welcome into our midst John Smith, who is
a child no longer. For two minutes, may we all
pray silently for the welfare of this young man.

*(The officiant places her hands above the head of the con-
secrant.)*

May you be blessed forever.
May the road before you be clear and light.
May you find your friends.
May you find your home.
May you find your talents.
May you bear your burdens.
May you know the joy of full contribution.
May He lift you up.
May He make His countenance to shine upon
      you.
May He guide your footsteps forever and forever.
Thank You, Lord.
We all say,
Amen.

Note: In the above ceremony, I made the consecrant's age thirteen. In reality, however, this ceremony should be done whenever the consecrant is ready, though no younger than twelve. That the consecrant be able to receive the ceremony of adulthood in full seriousness and sincerity is much more important than the time at which the rite is undertaken. Counseling is recommended if the consecrant needs help in achieving the inner conditions necessary for making this ceremony holy and real. In all ceremonial passages, the consciousness of those participating determines the power of the rite.

4

Ceremony of Marriage

OFFICIANT   Anne and John, I greet you.

To our assembled guests, on behalf of Anne and John, I welcome you. Anne and John, on behalf of those assembled here, I welcome you as well.

We welcome you to this moment in your lives and to the place you have come to in each other's hearts. We join with you on this day, as you commit before God and humanity that from this point forward you shall live as one.

I remind all of our guests that you have been invited here for a holy purpose, not just to witness, but to participate fully with your thoughts and prayers, asking God to bless this couple and their married life. You are here because this couple feels close to you and asks that you join with them in this dedication of sacred purpose. You represent symbolically all the people in the world who will be touched in any way by the life of this couple. You represent their friends and family, now and forever. They have chosen this act of marriage and this public, holy ceremony in which to proclaim it. Together we all thank God who brought them together and ask Him always to guide their way.

(*To the couple*)

Anne and John, we live at a time when very little in life is considered sacred. One thing must remain so, however, or all the world disintegrates. That is and shall be, an agreement between two people. This day we celebrate a sacred agreement between the two of you.

I congratulate you on the journey of your lives, on the strength and the courage it has taken for each of you to make your way to this place. Both of you have found a way to put away childish things and embrace a very serious love. You receive on this day the blessings thereof, for yourselves and all the world.

We live in times that are beset with problems. This marriage is not to be an escape from the world, but indeed it is to be a commitment to greater service to the world. You shall not exclude the world but include it in your love. Together, in this marriage, you shall contribute more fully, for you shall be more full.

Anne, John is God's gift to you, but he is not a gift for you alone. It is God's will that in your love, this man might find within himself a greater sense of who he is meant to be. You are asked by God to see the good in this man, to accept him for who he is and who he shall be, that thus he might be healed and made strong. In this way, God's purpose shall be accomplished in this relationship. May this man find, literally, the kingdom of heaven through the love you share.

And so it is with you also, John, that although Anne is God's gift to you, she is not a gift intended for you alone. You are asked by God to so love this woman, that in your love she might find herself as God has created her, so beautiful and strong and brave and true, that the entire world might be blessed by the presence of a woman who shines so. May she relax in your arms as she has never relaxed before. May she know, from now on, that there is one on whose love she can depend forever.

Our prayer for both of you is that you might find in each other's love such profound acceptance and total release, that together you might experience the forgiveness that shall free the world. May you create, with God, a piece of heaven on earth. Into a darkened world the Lord has sent your love for one another, and accomplishes between you, the miracle that will heal us all.

From this point forward, Anne, John's needs will carry the same priority as your own. Likewise, John, from this point forward, Anne's needs will be seen to be as important as your own. You shall not be as two conflicting or competing forces, but rather the energies of your lives shall blend into harmony and oneness through the grace of God. The angels shall dance between you, and they will rejoice in the dance of life you do together.

To both of you, I enjoin you to release at this time all impediments to your joy. In this moment may you forgive each other any past transgressions, that you might enter this marriage reborn. Allow the waters of forgiveness to wash you clean. You are given the chance to begin your lives again this day, as God grants you radical renewal through the power of this commitment. You commit to a compelling future for yourselves, for any children you have or might one day have, and to any part you might play in the healing of the world. Receive fully God's gifts on this day, as He receives so fully the gift of your love for each other. May you rejoice in Him, as He rejoices in you.

(To the parents)

To the parents of Anne and John, congratulations on the part you have played in raising a daughter and son of such serious purpose. They accept a very mature and meaningful task in taking on this marriage. On their behalf, and on behalf of all those here, I thank you. I remind you that it is more than their blood that is joined here; it is yours as well. With this marriage, God joins your two families, and it is the family unit that shall rebuild the world. With this in mind, I ask you, Anne's parents, to take this man, John, as your son. I ask your family to take him into their hearts, as son and brother, and beloved to Anne.

(*If necessary:* I ask that you forgive him any past transgressions, as I ask him also to forgive you yours.) May a great and glorious light sanctify this joining.

And of you, John's parents, I ask the same. I ask that you take this woman, Anne, into your hearts, that she might live from this day as your daughter. I ask your other children as well to receive her as their sister, for she is dear and beloved to your son, and shall be so, through the grace of God, to all your family. (*If necessary:* I ask that you forgive her any past transgressions, as I ask her also to forgive you yours.) May the miracle of this marriage extend throughout your family.

I would also like to ask at this time if anyone else has a problem with this marriage, because after today, please keep it quiet! As of this ceremony, may your tongues be still and utter only the positive, that your energies might support these two, that any words you say might bless and protect the holiness of this bond.

Anne, I now ask you to say publicly any declaration of commitment you'd like to make to John at this time.

(She does.)

John, I now ask you to say publicly any declaration of commitment you'd like to make to Anne at this time.

(He does.)

And so we come, Anne and John, to the presentation of rings by which you symbolize and bind your love.

Anne, please repeat after me:

With this ring,
I give to you my promise that from this day forward you shall not walk alone.
May my heart be your shelter
And my arms be your home.
May God bless you always.
May we walk together through all things.
May you feel deeply loved, for indeed you are.
May you always see your innocence in my eyes.
With this ring,
I give you my heart.
I have no greater gift to give.
I promise I shall do my best.
I shall always try.
I feel so honored to call you husband.

I feel so blessed to call you mine.
May we feel this joy forever.
I thank God.
I thank you.
Amen.

John, please repeat after me:

With this ring,
I give to you my promise that from this day for-
    ward you shall not walk alone.
May my heart be your shelter
And my arms be your home.
May God bless you always.
May we walk together through all things.
May you feel deeply loved, for indeed you are.
May you always see your innocence in my eyes.
With this ring,
I give you my heart.
I have no greater gift to give.
I promise I shall do my best.
I shall always try.
I feel so honored to call you my wife.
I feel so blessed to call you mine.
May we feel this joy forever.

I thank God.
I thank you.
Amen.

I'd now like to ask all of you to pray with me:

Dear God,
Please bless this couple.
May their love be nurtured by You, always and
    forever.
May this marriage be held in Your hands and
    ministered unto by Your angels.
We dedicate this love to You.
May it serve Your purposes; may it increase
    Your dominion.
May this man grow strong in the arms of this
    woman.
May this woman grow glorious in the love of
    this man.
May the earth be brought closer to heaven
    through this love.
May all the world be blessed hereby.
Thank You very much.
Amen.

Anne and John, I remind you that the God who brought you together and nurtured this relationship is the key to your success as a married couple. May you allow into your marriage the presence of a mystical third, who shall guide your thinking and bless your home. Call on Him consistently and often. We bring to mind as well the lives of any children who might one day gather unto you, and in the spirit of this day, we bless them also.

May this marriage be your sanctuary, your haven from worldly pain.

Anne, do you take this man, John, to be your lawful wedded husband, to love him and to honor him, nurture and sustain him, through times of darkness as well as light, henceforth and forevermore? Do you promise that times of trouble will not deter you, or tempt you to forsake this love? Do you commit before God to honor this vow unto all your days?

BRIDE I do.

OFFICIANT John, do you take this woman, Anne, to be your lawful wedded wife, to love her and cherish her, honor and sustain her, through times of darkness as well as light, henceforth and forevermore? Do you promise that times of trouble will not deter you, or tempt you to forsake this love? Do you commit before God to honor this vow unto all your days?

GROOM   I do.

OFFICIANT   And now, Anne and John, by the authority vested in me by the state of New York, but much more important, by the authority vested in me by the fact that I believe in the power of your agreement this day, the look of love in your eyes, and the seriousness with which you make this commitment; and because I believe my faith is shared by others gathered here, it is my honor and my delight to now pronounce you husband and wife.

Ladies and gentlemen, Mr. and Mrs. (*name*)!

5

Ceremony of the Elder:
A Rite of Midlife

As a generation, we are growing into our wisdom. We are hungry for our wise women, our wise men. We are hungry to know them and to become them. The wise have seen the light at the center of things, and the light at the center of things is who we are. Until we see that, the mission of our lives remains unfulfilled.

This rite is very significant when done for someone's fiftieth, sixtieth, or seventieth birthday. It should also be noted that it is as appropriate for men as it is for women.

OFFICIANT We gather on this day to celebrate an important passage in the life of Anne Martin. She is to us a beloved child of God. She is as well the daughter of (*name*) and (*name*), the wife of (*name*), the mother of (*names*), and sister to the world.

The years of her life on earth have brought her to this sacred moment, where she takes upon herself, through the grace of God, the mantle of the Elder. From this day forward, she celebrates and carries forth the purpose of the wise ones, who oversee our human progress, who nurture and sustain us. She shall be grandmother to all children, handmaiden to God and Goddess, revered for her insights and honored for her knowledge.

To you, Anne, having lived these years, having seen what you have seen and cried the tears of troubled times, we now acknowledge that you have climbed the ladder of the elder ones. May God reveal to you a sacred sensibility. We are blessed by your presence. We are grateful to know you.

Please reveal to us your story.

> (*Anne has prepared, prior to the ceremony, a letter to the world. It describes her history however she cares to reveal it. She forgives and blesses past times. She offers herself for continued service to humanity and to the world. She claims the full blessings of her maturity,*

the value of her experience to now share in faith and inspiration with those who seek her counsel.)

And so it is. We thank you, Anne.

I'd like to ask any gathered here who wish to at this time to share with us your acknowledgments of Anne, and your prayers for her life in the future.

(They do.)

Now I ask those assembled here to join with me in prayers for this woman:

Dear God,
We thank you for the years gone by, and we
thank you for the years ahead.
This woman has lived, dear Lord.
She has seen the cycles of life and death.
She has rejoiced at morning and mourned its
passing.
Thus she has now gained sacred knowledge:
The power to heal through the depth of her
compassion;
The power to teach through the depth of her
understanding;
The power to bring forth a new and better
world through the depth of her vision.

May all now see in her, and may she see within
  herself, the elder, the wise one, the one who
  holds the candle of illumination for all the
  world to see.
May she be honored and revered.
May her heart be as a womb to new life.
May her children's children see the power of the
  ages as it is written in her eyes.
She has arrived, dear Lord.
May she be blessed.
She has come so far.
May she now know peace.
She has worked so hard.
May she now find rest.
And may a cycle now begin for her, more pow-
  erful than any other, most glorious of all.
For she is now the fullness of human, of
  woman, of God's servant and child.
Bless her always.
May she shine.
Amen.

I would like to ask you all now to join with me
in two minutes of silent prayer, in thanksgiving
and in blessing on this woman.
  (They do so.)

And now, Anne, I'd like to ask you to read to us your vision for us and for this world.

(She does so.)

Anne, please repeat after me:

Dear God,
Thank You for my life.
May it open now to a new and glorious chapter.
May my past and future be transformed.
May I become a channel for good as never before.
May the generation behind me receive strength
    and comfort from my being here.
May I glorify and fortify Your light on earth.
Amen.

OFFICIANT   Dear Anne, you are to be honored and respected for what you have done and who you are. You are an Elder among us, a wise one who has seen what we have not seen. Teach us, that we might all be more.

We deeply thank you. We wish you well. Go in peace and go in joy.

(To those assembled)

I bless you all.

Amen.

6

Ceremony of Divorce

The purpose of this ceremony is to heal hearts, by forgiving the past and releasing the future. This rite is to be held in the presence of the couple's children, and one person chosen by the couple to be the officiant of the ceremony.

Like all the ceremonies presented here, this one should not be taken lightly or done casually. I recommend that a spiritual counselor or therapist be the officiant, after having worked with the couple privately to ensure that both participants are ready to declare publicly their forgiveness and release.

OFFICIANT   We come together today not in joy, but in acceptance.

For yourselves and for your children, we ask God's help in this important transition. May you release each other in love and forgiveness, that you may go on from this point healed and whole, no longer married but family still.

We join with you in God's presence, as you hereby let go the bond of marriage between you. We ask God's blessing on you, as you both seek and grant forgiveness. We join with you in the recognition that through the grace of God there are no endings but only the chance for new beginnings, and we pray this day for God to give that new beginning, to you and to you children.

I say to the children of this couple, whose souls are tried by the experience of this divorce, or have perhaps been tried still more by the condition of your parents' marriage: May the angels minister unto your hearts and free you from your pain. May you forgive your parents. In your hearts, may you accept and bless this decision.

> *(The officiant now asks the children, one by one, if there is any statement of feeling or intention that they would like to make. The children do so.)*

And so it is. Let us pray.

Dear God,
We ask You to take these two dearly beloved
   souls into Your hands.
Include in Your mercy and compassion their
   children.
May the golden cord that has bound these
   two in marriage be not violently severed,
   but carefully and peacefully laid aside, this
   act forgiven and granted meaning by God
   Himself.
May these two remain parents and sacred
   friends forever.
Never shall the bond of marriage be made
   meaningless, before God or humankind.
May these two beloved children of God remember that the love of their union was important, and honor it always.
Your experiences together were the lessons of
   lives lived searching for love.
God understands.
He asks you to remember the innocence in each
   other, now and forever.
May forgiveness wash you clean.

The love you gave and the love you received
were real and will be with you always.
The rest, let us silently and willingly give to
God, that He might heal your hearts and give
rest to your souls.
You have suffered enough, in coming to this
point.
With this prayer, may your family begin again,
having released the past and sought from
God Himself a new path forward.
We place both past and future in the hands of
God.
You are still a family, blessed and held together
by God.
May you remain so forever.
And so it is.
Amen.

> *(At this point, the couple may choose a ceremonial
> return of each other's wedding rings or some other
> symbolic gesture of loving release. In marriage cere-
> monies, a couple often chooses to light a single candle
> from two separate ones. In the divorce ceremony, a
> couple may choose to light two separate candles from
> one. This symbolizes that although they shall now lead*

*two separate lives, the fire at the centers of their beings
were blended by God and shall remain so forever.)*

DIVORCING HUSBAND *(To wife)* *(Name)*, I bless
you and release you. Please forgive me. I forgive
you. Go in peace. You remain in my heart through
the grace of God.

DIVORCING WIFE *(To husband)* *(Name)*, I bless
you and release you. Please forgive me. I forgive
you. Go in peace. You remain in my heart through
the grace of God.

OFFICIANT   Please repeat after me:

Dear God,
Please help us now.
Bless this decision.
Bless our children.
Thank You for what has been.
Thank You for what shall be.
Amen.

I now ask all those gathered here for two minutes of silent prayer for the healing and restora-
tion of these wounded hearts.

(They do so.)

And so it is. (*Name*) and (*name*), you are released from your commitment of marriage. You remain committed forever to the bonds of goodwill.

God bless you and bless your children.

Amen.

7

Memorial Service

OFFICIANT   We come together on this day to remember the life, both temporal and eternal, of one whom we have loved dearly. As brother, son, lover, husband, and father, John has lived in our hearts and shall live there forever.

We release what was and make room for what shall be, as we testify within our minds that life does not end but merely transmutes, that today we say good-bye and yet we also say hello. We say good-bye to the physical focus of our relationship with this man, and greet the relationship with his soul that now begins anew. Through the grace of God, the dead do not die. They live forever, in God's mind and in ours.

And so it is that our service today is twofold: We are here to release what has been, the very human dramas of our love for this man, our shared stories, our histories. Yet we also open our hearts today, that our relationships with him might be reborn through the grace of God. Whom God hath given to us, no one and nothing can take away. Whom He brings together shall be together unto all eternity. For God is more powerful than death. We celebrate not the crucifixion of this worldly passing, although we certainly allow ourselves to feel its sting. Rather, we celebrate the resurrection by which John and we shall yet live forever.

Let us pray:

Dear God,
We pray for the spirit of John, our beloved son and brother and husband and friend.
Take him into Your arms, dear Lord, and bring peace to his soul.
May his transition be sweet.
We see at this time all of the beloved people who mourn him.
And we watch as a glorious angel of God now ties the golden cord of eternal life at one end

to John's heart and at the other end to the
heart of everyone who so receives him.

And now the angel places his hands on this
cord, signaling the power of God, which
blesses and sustains us, and holds firm our
relationships, through life and through death.

We receive into our hearts the truth of God's
eternal life.

Through the glory of God and the mercy of
God and the majesty of God, may love still
live forever and forever.

Please uphold us through this sorrow and this
loss, as we grieve and release this one we
loved and shall so sorely miss.

Dearly beloved God,

Be our strength at this time, that we might yet
see the truth of the world as You created it,

That there is no death, that John still lives, and
in You we still live with him.

Thank You very much.

Amen.

(To parents)

I'd like to say to the parents of this man, that our
hearts go with you. You are to be commended
that you raised such a beautiful son. I hope the

presence of the people who are here today proves to you the high regard in which he is held in this community. He made a difference. He touched our hearts. Our prayer is that your grief might move through you gently. May you hold in your minds forever the truth we agree upon here today: John yet lives in the arms and in the mind of God. Keep your hearts and minds open to receive him. He shall yet communicate his love for you, for he lives on in spirit and shall not forget you.

(To a spouse)

I know that you feel you will never be the same, and you will not. You will be harder or you will be softer. Our prayer for you is that you not give in to the dark side of sorrow but rather let its light illumine you. Sorrow can stretch your heart now, and more light shine there than ever before. Your bond with John was neither temporal nor temporary. You were joined in holy bond, and thus your bond lives forever. Receive him in death as you received him in life. John shall live as an angel on your shoulder. He shall watch over you and protect you and send to you all manner of good. Be faithful unto God that you might know the realms of which I speak. There are more ways to know a man than just by the senses of the physical world. May your heart and eyes stay open. John shall come to you still and be a blessing on you always.

He has gone before you to prepare with God a heavenly home in which you both shall dwell when the time is right. Until that day, be patient and endure. You are very loved. God is with you. The adventure ahead is not dark but light.

(To young children)

To you, John's children, we say this: If we could have done anything to keep your father with you, we would have. It is our deepest sorrow that he is not here now. And yet, may you remember throughout your lives that your father was a wonderful man. He was strong and brave and good and wise. And his spirit will be with you forever. He will be as an angel who watches over you and a force of love that always protects you. You will grow up to be like him, for his spirit remains with you. Although you are left with no father on earth, truly you have two now, in heaven. They love you, and so do we.

(The officiant asks if there is anyone who would like to share thoughts or feelings about John. They do so.)

And now please join with me in prayer once more. If there is any unforgiveness left between you and John, use this time and place to heal what only God can heal.

We see in the middle of our minds a little ball
   of golden light.
We watch now as this light expands, until it
   covers the entire inner vision of our minds
We see, within this light, a beautiful temple.
There is a garden that surrounds the temple
   and a body of water that flows through the
   garden.
The inside of the temple is filled as well by this
   golden light.
And we are here, for we have been brought here
   together by the power and in the presence of
   God.
We invite to join us here, at the center of this
   light, God's most beautiful angel, however it
   appears to us.
(To some of us here, he appears as Jesus.)

And now we see the soul of John, our husband
   and brother and son and friend, relax into
   the arms of God.

We see a golden cord that connects him to all
   of us, our hearts now tied to his forever.

We watch the angel put this cord to our hearts,
   and now we commune with the spirit of John.

Let us say to him what we need to say and hear
   from him what we need to hear.

May we say to God what we need to say and
   hear from Him what we need to hear.

John, we love you.

We thank you for all you have been to us.

We release you to God, that your journey ahead
   may be glorious and sweet.

(Let there now be one minute of silence.)

Dear God, please take Your servant.

Dear God, please take our pain.

Thank You very much.

And so it is.

Amen.

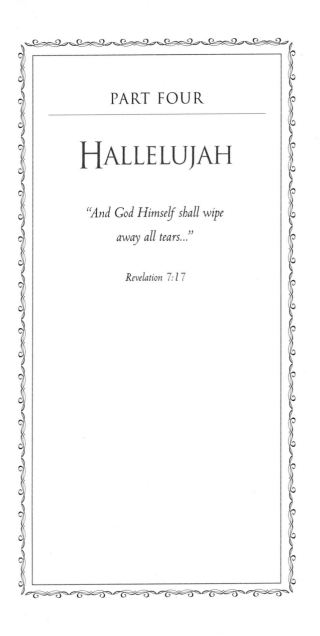

PART FOUR

HALLELUJAH

*"And God Himself shall wipe
away all tears..."*

Revelation 7:17

Rapture

A quickening pulse, an open door, a mystery now beckons us. It whispers, Fly forth free. Recast your shame and now be proud. Who, we wonder, whispers thus? Who, indeed, is there, and knows me well, behind that door?

It matters and it doesn't, who it is. It is living. Soft. Fierce. It awaits us, the appointed time, 10, 9, 8, 7, 6, 5, 4, 3 . . . He comes now. Softly, gently, like a lover, which he is. He knows each hair and secret, every butterfly and tortured cry. Quantum physics is child's play to him; your slightest pain is more important.

He isn't who you thought he was. He isn't a was; he is an is. He isn't bound by stupid projections. He's at least as smart as you are.

God sent me. God sent me. Hate the guy. Hate the guy. What an amazing drama that, to blast away the one who knows, the one who cares, the one who loves. And yet we do, we have not stopped. He can't come back, although he's here. We blew it then. We'd blow it now. In fact, we blow it constantly.

Over and over, we lie, we steal, we hurt, we kill, and yet there are those gentle winds. They form a wave of love's resistance, the invitation to be reborn, to find that man behind the door, to find his arms, to see his eyes. He doesn't look like anyone. He doesn't look like us.

And yet he is. He is us. The whole thing. The big picture. The new, the old. The answer. The hope. And you don't have to join a religion. You don't have to believe in him. You don't have to believe what I say. You can do whatever you want. But he is here. And he has power. And he has desire. To set you free.

He's going to. It's happening. Your skin is changing, your head is dancing, your eyes are seeing what they didn't see. Admit it, darling. Your mind is blown. He blew some bubbles into your brain. He did. He did. I saw he did.

I saw him first when I couldn't stand it. Couldn't stand the sleepless nights. And he just sat there, on the *end of my bed, and he looked at me. And I knew it was him. And now I see him everywhere.*

And so do you. He's picking up speed. He's bursting forth. And so are you. And so are we. The race is on.

The old boy has a bicycle. We're on the back; he's headed out. Out of all this stuff we made, disappointingly misdirected. We call it life but it isn't life. It's a mockery, it's blasphemy. You know this. I know this. One bold gesture and we're outta here.

He has a mother. You knew that. She's beautiful in ways so sweet. She's not the kind we often see. She's not the kind we see at all. She fusses and she fixes us. You thought maybe that we don't need fixing? Oh, please, with that. We're a total teardown.

And that's the beauty of the current day. They're going to remodel us. They told me so. They told a trillion others too, in case you think I think my ears are special. I know they're not, but they are unplugged, at least compared to how they used to be. And I hear music. Yours and mine.

He climbs a staircase. At the top of the stairs is a small, sparse room. He opens the door and says to us, Stay here. I will be back. I will bring you gifts. Try them out in here. And when you leave, you will head back down. Wear your new clothes. Take your gifts. They'll never know we had such fun, until they do, and then we'll all have fun together. This isn't bad. It's a total party.

A total party. That's the universe. That's the joke. A total party. A total joy.

Praise the Lord, our reign is over. We did enough damage. Our prince is come.

And now, about her. Oh, you say, you mean the slut? Yes. The slut. How dare you call her that? He kissed her on the mouth. So there, you bastards. He did. He did. He embraced her love; he embraces her still. Her charms were good, their kisses sweet. You can't stand it. But you don't know.

She saw it all. She knew it all. Oil on his body. Kisses on his hands.

Darling, come. Hide no more. Run no more. Seek no more. Cry no more. Hit no more. Yearn no more. Prove no more. Destroy no more. Defend no more. Attack no more. Relax. Come here I'm here I'm here I'm here I'm here I'm here I'm here I'm here I'm here.

He's in front of the door. He's behind the door. He is the door.

He is.

AMEN

ACKNOWLEDGMENTS

Thank you to my parents for your unwavering support, and with my apologies for the fact that I *still* don't want to go to law school.

My deep thanks to Harry Evans for the precious space and freedom in which to develop as a writer.

Many thanks to Al Lowman and Alan Weil for being my brothers, giving me support and protection through both mountains and valleys.

Thanks to Andrea Cagan for being such a marvelous midwife to my writing.

Thanks to Mitchell Ivers for being an outstanding and sympathetic editor.

Thank you to my dear friends Rich Cooper, Norma Ferrara, Ed Schneck, Carrie Williams, Linda Ford, Minda Burr, Victoria Pearman, and Sandy Scott for continued kindness, help and listening. Without you, forget it . . .

Thanks to Ashley Sibille and Wendy Breakstone for excellent assistance and understanding. Thanks also to John Ravena, Scott Uhl, David Gordon, Hal Sparks, Don Thompson, Todd Schroeder and Ryane

McAuliffe. I very much appreciate the help I receive from all of you.

Thank you to Dan Stone and Rich Coppedge, who are not here but who really are.

And to you, my darling Emma, you are Mommy's most precious, most beautiful angel. You are totally beyond the beyond the beyond. Thanks for every little hair on your gorgeous little head.

I remember you, Jane . . .

*An extensive library of Marianne Williamson's
ongoing live lectures is available on audio cassette
and may be ordered only by calling toll-free
800-982-9863.*